It's About Tyme
. . . .

This book is dedicated to those who see the world as it is and find a way to make it better.

It's About Tyme

Banking Beyond Borders

Adrian Saville and Bruce Whitfield

MACMILLAN

First published in 2025
by Pan Macmillan South Africa
Private Bag X19
Northlands
Johannesburg
2116

www.panmacmillan.co.za

ISBN 978-1-77010-983-4
e-ISBN 978-1-77010-984-1

© Adrian Saville and Bruce Whitfield 2025
From TIME © 2025 TIME USA LLC. All rights reserved. Used under license.

All rights reserved. No part of this publication may be reproduced, stored in or introduced into a retrieval system, or transmitted, in any form or by any means (electronic, mechanical, photocopying, recording or otherwise), without the prior written permission of the publisher. Any person who does any unauthorised act in relation to this publication may be liable to criminal prosecution and civil claims for damages.

Editing by Sally Hines
Proofreading by Sean Fraser
Design and typesetting by Triple M Design, Johannesburg
Cover design by publicide

Contents

Abbreviations and Acronyms vi
Preface: This Ain't No Fairy Tale vii

Part I: Before Tyme

1 The Quiet Contract 3
2 The Wrong Plus-One 12

Part II: The Ideas That Shaped Tyme

3 From Branches to Backends 25
4 Hidden in Plain Sight 39

Part III: The First Tyme

5 When Two Worlds Collide 51
6 A Pure Digital Plan 65
7 Holding on for Dear Life 71

Part IV: The Second Tyme

8 The Phygital Frontier 89
9 217 Calls, the Pawnshop King and the Ticking Time Bomb 100
10 Building the Tyme Machine 114
11 Going Beyond Borders 133
12 Back from the Edge 151
13 This Tyme Is Different 169
14 Knighted in the Global Court of Fintech 172
15 Here's to the Crazy Ones 178

Notes 194
Acknowledgements 202

Abbreviations and Acronyms

AI	artificial intelligence
ARC	African Rainbow Capital
ASEAN	Association of Southeast Asian Nations
BEE	Black Economic Empowerment
BNPL	buy now, pay later
BSP	Bangko Sentral ng Pilipinas
CBA	Commonwealth Bank of Australia
DFI	digital financial inclusion
FRD	Foundation for Research Development
GDP	gross domestic product
GIBS	Gordon Institute of Business Science
GMV	gross merchandise value
IMF	International Monetary Fund
IPO	initial public offering
KYC	Know Your Customer
LeSS	Large-Scale Scrum
MSME	micro-, small- and medium-sized enterprise
NPS	net promoter score
SRC	Student Representative Council
SASSA	South African Social Security Agency
TFG	The Foschini Group
TYME	Take Your Money Everywhere
UK	United Kingdom
US	United States
USSD	Unstructured Supplementary Service Data
ZCC	Zion Christian Church

Preface

This Ain't No Fairy Tale

Hope is not the conviction that something will turn out well, but the certainty that something makes sense, regardless of how it turns out.
— Václav Havel

This book is about Tyme Group and its banks, whose rapid rise has made them one of the fastest-growing digital banks in the world. Most business biographies emerge when founders have nothing left to prove. They offer a comfortable, often-sanitised retrospective – typically centred on a single dominant figure and commissioned to enshrine a preferred legacy. The result is usually a self-congratulatory, occasionally dry narrative, softened by the selective misremembering of key events. Or they are otherwise a collection of fireside fables and late-evening tales that are anecdotal or perhaps only have meaning if you were there. These books tend to glorify the individual without whom the business would never have existed, painting a picture of triumph over adversity and innovation against the odds.

The best business books, however, go much further – interrogating character, motivation and the near failures along the way. Phil Knight's *Shoe Dog* stands apart.[1] Written in the first person, it delivers a raw, unvarnished account of the relentless struggle to build the global footwear and sportswear company Nike. It is a gripping reminder of how tough entrepreneurship really is and an antidote to the myth-making that dominates the genre.

By contrast, Howard Schultz's *Pour Your Heart into It* is a carefully coiffured tale of how Starbucks redefined coffee culture.[2] The book gives little space to the ruthless corporate strategies that played out behind the global expansion of the world's largest coffee house. Similarly, Richard Branson's ever-popular *Losing My Virginity* presents the success of the Virgin empire as the result of the swashbuckling adventures of a maverick, while skimming over some of the near disasters and many legal entanglements, which, if fully addressed, would make it a far more valuable book.[3] Both Schultz and Branson have built remarkable empires, make no mistake. But omitting the messiness – the moments of madness, near misses and true miscalculations – detracts from their achievements and diminishes the true value of these types of books.

There is a market hungry for stories of success and groundbreaking achievements. It is hard not to be captivated by the genius of Steve Jobs and the creation of Apple Inc., or the astounding accomplishments of Elon Musk and his various entities, including Tesla Inc., SpaceX and Neuralink. But critics of Walter Isaacson's biographies point out that while they are positioned as warts-and-all accounts, they often veer into awestruck admiration. It is the curse of the biographer. The worst of these books serve as corporate hagiographies – stories of singular geniuses, trailblazers, mavericks or lone wolves bending the world to their will, rather than complex portraits of ambition, failure, miscalculation, recovery, reinvention and perhaps even large doses of luck.

Take Microsoft, one of the most exalted businesses in modern history. Few realise that in the early 1990s, the company came close to abandoning Windows, cutting its support team to nearly zero before reversing course. As economist and author Paul Ormerod suggests, the line between success and failure is often razor-thin.[4] The real challenge lies in deciphering how much of that edge is shaped by skill, and how much is pure luck.

One dose of good luck for Tyme that felt like bad luck initially is also instructive. 'Tyme had received news that they had been given a licence in Pakistan,' says Varun Mittal, a prominent figure in Southeast Asia's fast-growing digital innovation landscape and the creator of Fintech Nation. 'They received a call to say prepare a press release. The next day the licences were announced and Tyme was not on the list – they had been outbid. As fortune would have it, if they had gone to Pakistan, instead of the Philippines, it is likely that they would never have raised money again with South Africa and Pakistan as the portfolio. Since then, Pakistan has had floods, natural disasters, a currency collapse and an IMF bailout.'

The real lessons for success often lie in what is left unsaid.

So, when Tyme Group co-founder Coenraad (Coen) Jonker approached the authors in early 2024 to write this book, there was a serious discussion to be had. Each of us was busy with new projects and neither of us wanted our reputations as independent thinkers to be sullied by the fact that this would be a paid-for project. Equally, however, we each had some insight into the tale, and we were more than curious – arguably intrigued – to learn more about what it took to build a multi-country digital bank for emerging markets that had evidence of extraordinary resilience and remarkable growth and, which we soon came to appreciate, was on the cusp of unicorn status.

Jonker was unequivocal: 'We are forgetting our own stories,' he said in our first meeting. 'We need to have the stories written down. And this book needs to tell our history and experiences, warts and all.' He believed there was a valuable story that needed to be told about the many close shaves, the paydays that were nearly missed, the bailouts, the rejections, the betrayals, the battles and the scores of frustrations that might have led to capitulation and failure many times over. Instead, there was a bigger underlying story that would eventually convince Brazil's Nubank – regarded globally as one of the world's most successful digital banks – to take a 10% stake in the business. This would drive the indicative value of Tyme to US$1.5 billion, giving it the technology world's cherished status of 'unicorn'.

The line between legacy banks, neobanks and digital banks is becoming increasingly blurred. Thanks to technological innovation, legacy banks are increasingly digitised; but by the nature of their long evolutions, they are burdened with systems and processes that slow down their growth trajectory relative to the unencumbered, more recent business models. The new generation founders argue digital banks give them a significant cost and agility advantage over their older competitors. One of the key debates in the industry is whether the legacy banks can speed up their digital transformation and evolve quickly enough to mitigate against the risk of being overtaken by the lower-cost, more nimble rivals.

The Nubank investment was made notwithstanding the fact that GoTyme in the Philippines was still some way off achieving profitability, and TymeBank in South Africa had only just started making money. But the milestones announced at the time of the transaction made it clear that this is a business that has already achieved remarkable success against the odds. Successes included acquiring 10 million customers in South Africa five years after launch, and 5 million customers in the Philippines a little over two years after starting – and the cumulative count was growing by about 400,000 new customers each month. And then there are the prospects being eyed in Indonesia and Vietnam – with a combined population of 385 million people. And what of a possible listing on a major stock exchange that has been proposed as early as 2028? It is a bold ambition because there are no guarantees that the group, or any of its banks, will survive that long in a fast-changing global environment. But, as we have come to learn in researching this book, bold ambition is Tyme's style.

Building a hyper-scalable, unified banking platform – one that can navigate the complexities of industry infrastructure, satisfy regulators across multiple jurisdictions and deliver a markedly better customer experience than what exists in markets around the world – is nothing short of a mammoth undertaking. Even those who admire what has been achieved so far remain cautious as to whether this can be done in a way that makes it more attractive than the incumbents in its target market and at a price point that makes it viable.

The ever-present risk of damaging regulatory intervention was vividly illustrated in July 2025 when South Africa's Department of Home Affairs unilaterally imposed a 6,500% increase on the long-standing 15c fee it had charged since 2013 for real-time digital identity verifications – a service used by banks, retailers and fintechs to onboard customers. The fee jumped to R10 per real-time check, with an additional R10 charge applied for verification confirmation, effectively raising the cost of a single transaction to R20 in some cases. Home Affairs defended the move as a long-overdue correction after years of underinvestment, arguing that the increased revenue would fund a vastly upgraded system with sub-second response times and near perfect reliability, thereby protecting national identity infrastructure.

Tyme strongly opposed the sudden hike, warning that it could undermine financial inclusion by rendering some low-fee banking models unviable – especially for grant recipients and informal workers. The bank argued that a public verification system, already funded by taxpayers, should not be transformed into a revenue-generating venture to offset state inefficiencies. Home Affairs Minister Leon Schreiber remained defiant, accusing Tyme of 'faux outrage' and insisting that the pricing reform was essential for security and digital governance. At the time of writing, several players across South Africa's credit and fintech sectors were exploring legal avenues and technological alternatives to challenge the fee structure and push for a more sustainable solution.

When you consider the potential risks to the model on top of what has gone wrong in getting Tyme to this point in its relatively short history, and you count the times the business has teetered on the brink of failure, there can be no promise that the firm will survive. But what if they do get it right and deliver a model that makes it possible for the 24% of the world's population currently excluded from the financial system to get access to affordable banking? What if they grow their retail banking operation, which has the lowest customer acquisition cost in the world, into new markets at scale? What if their brazen ambition translates into a multi-country banking group with 100 million customers, and a return on equity that is double the industry's long-term average?

One banking analyst questioned whether it was not too early to be writing this story. We don't think so. In that lies the courage of this business biography – a willingness for the story to be told regardless of the outcome, and we hope with at least a hint of the same courage as the founders, Coenraad Jonker and Tjaart van der Walt, and the people who put their faith into the co-founders' vision. In writing this book, we are willing to be called out for being wrong when hindsight strikes. But having conducted an exhaustive set of interviews and met with everyone from co-founders to coders and regulators to denouncers, we believe we are telling the story of a firm that is playing a central part in reshaping one of the world's most important, and oldest, industries.

Having immersed ourselves in the granular detail of Tyme, scouring public and private datasets, carrying out scores of interviews and visiting operations and offices in all the countries where the group has a presence – the Philippines, Singapore, South Africa and Vietnam – we are in no doubt that there are easier ways to make money than building a multi-country bank across time zones, cultures and regulatory systems, bringing an unparalleled level of complexity to play.

But who wants to read the story of 'easy'?

As authors, we have had to be mindful of falling into the trap of drinking the Kool-Aid. Jonker is objectively, and by any global measure, a charismatic and inspiring founder, described by one former staff member as having a 'messianic quality'.

In the words of David Pfaff, co-chief executive officer at Tyme, 'Coen is transparent, open, with the most incredible EQ, always interested in the best for you. His knowledge of the industry is off the charts. He is able to sell the dream; smart, trustworthy and incredibly generous. He knows how to sprinkle fairy dust.'

Jonker has pushed a core team to consistently perform at the limits of their ability in a relentless drive to reimagine, re-engineer and reinvent one of the world's oldest industries. If, in writing this book, we have fallen into the same traps that we have criticised here, then we apologise in advance. Accepting that risk, we believe that this is a story that must be told.

It is also not just Jonker or Van der Walt's story. That would be easier to tell, but it would ultimately take you into the realm of those we have challenged earlier in this preface. An ideal business biography strikes a balance between insight and storytelling. It must be brutally honest – no sugar-coating of failures, inflating successes or confusing skill with luck.

The best business books unpack the psychology of leadership, showing what drives decision-making under pressure. Context matters: economic shifts, competitive landscapes and personal struggles must be woven into this tale seamlessly because they don't happen independently; they happen while the founders sleep, shareholders revolt or regulators react.

A great business biography doesn't just celebrate achievements – it dissects them, revealing the vision, good fortune, timing and sheer grit involved. It should be as much a cautionary tale as an inspiration. Above all, it must be compelling – less a corporate curriculum vitae; more a gripping, real-world case study in risk, resilience and reinvention.

We believe this book delivers on this.

We could have called it: 'How a bunch of people who may very well be certifiable are trying to build a bank from scratch in the hardest way possible across borders, narrowly avoiding catastrophe at every turn, but waking up every day to keep doing it …' But the publishers warned that title was too long. So, instead, we think the right title is simpler: 'It's About Tyme'.

Part I

Before Tyme

Chapter 1

The Quiet Contract

The privilege of a lifetime is to become who you truly are.
— Carl Jung

Coenraad Jonker remembers the exact moment the first seed of what would become Tyme was planted.

It was the year 2000. The 30-something-year-old lawyer, newly appointed CEO of what was to become Africa's largest corporate law firm, Edward Nathan, was among the first cohort of MBA students at the newly built Gordon Institute of Business Science (GIBS). The ochre-painted walls of the Illovo campus in Johannesburg were still drying as the founder and dean, Nick Binedell, welcomed bright-eyed students – recruited with little more than a plastic scale model and an infectious ambition to shape future business leaders.

'It was a form of careful seduction,' Binedell recalls. 'We attracted people on the "why" rather than the "how" of what we aimed to achieve.'

That 'why' proved pivotal for Jonker. During a macroeconomics class, he noticed a copy of the *Financial Times* open to a review of a book titled *The Mystery of Capital* by Peruvian economist Hernando de Soto. The book addressed a question Coen had been grappling with: South Africa had won political emancipation in 1994, but economic freedom remained elusive for millions. It was a book that was to elicit a hobby that would develop into an obsession and culminate in a dramatic career change, which would lead to the creation of Tyme – a digital-first bank leveraging retail partnerships to serve those on the fringes of the mainstream economy.

South Africa was the perfect incubator. The country had capitalised on post-1994 goodwill, Nelson Mandela had stepped aside after his first term as promised, and Thabo Mbeki's market-driven policies were showing results. Yet millions still fell through the cracks.

Binedell remembers Jonker well: 'He was quiet, thoughtful, sensitive even. Philosophical, smart, incisive. All the faculty rated him highly, and he has used those qualities to full effect.' Jonker joined the MBA programme to learn about business. He had excelled academically, earning top marks in both his undergraduate and LLB degrees at the University of the Free State in the early 1990s. Known for his sharp legal mind, his partners recognised other skills in him, too. He found himself at the helm of the country's top corporate law firm, managing a difficult partnership between some of the smartest, most independent legal minds of the time and Nedcor, the banking group that had bought the business in a deal that was not working for either party.

It was a formidable task. Lawyers, after all, were not accustomed to taking instructions from anyone but their high-paying clients. But Jonker was no stranger to navigating complexity, or to challenging the status quo. His unconventional upbringing had prepared him well.

By the age of 15, he had attended eight schools across seven towns. His parents, too, had never been ones for convention. His father, Gert, a theologian, taught Hebrew and the Old Testament at the University of Zululand before leaving academia to become a NG Kerk dominee (Dutch Reformed Church minister). A scholar at heart, Gert continued studying philosophy and theology, mastering eight languages, including ancient texts such as Aramaic.

From Pretoria to Empangeni, then Durban's working-class Bluff, and later Da Gama Park near Simon's Town Naval Base, the Jonker family moved frequently. It was in Da Gama Park that young Coenraad met Phillip Oliver, a newly arrived British immigrant whose father, an ex-Royal Navy officer, had relocated to South Africa.

The dominee's household was warm and welcoming, and Phillip remembers the young Coenraad fondly: 'He had an impish grin, and a gentle, thoughtful demeanour. He was quirky, original and always up for whatever game I'd just invented.' The boys spent hours playing in the dunes and skateboarding through the quiet streets. One afternoon, Phillip recalls a mishap that left him with a bruised foot. 'Coen's usual mischievous expression changed instantly to deep concern. He helped me limp inside, calling for his mother, Alida. Her solution? A cup of rooibos tea in a delicate china cup. As I wrinkled my nose at the unfamiliar smell, Coen reassured me, "You will like it." He was easy to trust.'

In their endless childhood roleplays, there was always a moment when one of them lay 'mortally wounded' or 'gasping their last'. That was Coenraad's time to shine. Clasping his hands together, screwing up his eyes, he would solemnly recount all the virtues of the fallen, pleading with the Almighty to take pity and bring swift healing.

By age ten, the Jonker family was back in Pretoria, where Coenraad attended two more schools before the family finally settled in Bloemfontein, South Africa's judicial capital. His mother, who had once pursued a career in the performing arts, had set aside her ambitions to focus on being a dominee's wife. But she later returned to teaching, making a daily two-hour round trip to Thaba Nchu in the nominally independent homeland of Bophuthatswana to teach English and Afrikaans. Despite the widespread resistance to Afrikaans as a medium of education, as it was regarded as the language of the oppressor during the volatile 1980s, she took pride in the fact that none of her students failed either subject.

The Jonkers were often stationed in poorer, ultra-conservative Afrikaner communities, many of which were gripped by fear as violent opposition to apartheid intensified. Coenraad's upbringing was more open-minded than most. His father challenged convention within the Church, at one point arguing – despite fierce opposition and personal risk – that homosexuals should be welcomed and embraced by the Church.

In Bloemfontein, the teenage Jonker attended Sentraal High School, the lesser-known Afrikaans counterpart to the prestigious, dual-medium Grey

PART I: BEFORE TYME

College. Grey, famous for producing generations of sports stars – including disgraced cricket captain Hansie Cronjé and Olympic swimmer Ryk Neethling – had a towering reputation. Sentraal, by contrast, was more academically and culturally focused, although it had its own claim to fame in Zola Budd, the barefoot runner best remembered for her collision with Mary Decker-Slaney at the 1984 Los Angeles Olympics.

Jonker's father would drop him off at school in the mornings, parting with the phrase *carpe diem* (Latin for 'seize the day'), later made famous by actor Robin Williams in *Dead Poets Society*. It left the teenager in awe of the array of new opportunities that were open to him every day.

Later, at the University of the Free State, Jonker found his voice amid the country's shifting political landscape. As a second-year law student, he was persuaded by students in that faculty to run for the Student Representative Council (SRC), then dominated by conservative theology students. Campus politics was fraught – black students were allowed to study there only by government dispensation and faced long commutes due to apartheid-era segregation, which forbade their staying at the university overnight. Bloemfontein was notorious for the nightly siren signalling the 9pm curfew, which would sound to give a 15-minute warning to any black person to take shelter or vacate areas reserved for whites only. It could be heard across the city and the consequences for any black person found on the street after that time were dire and transgressors faced arrest. The ruling National Party still held sway on campus, the far-right Afrikaner Weerstandsbeweging (AWB) was gaining traction and tension simmered. It was in this context that Jonker successfully campaigned for the racial integration of the university residences on campus.

In February 1990, President F.W. de Klerk, under mounting global pressure, unbanned liberation movements and released political prisoners. But at the University of the Free State, change was slower to take hold. Determined to shift the tide, Jonker made a phone call that would alter not only the course of his own life, but that of Tjaart van der Walt, the chair of the Stellenbosch SRC.

Stellenbosch, long a training ground for National Party politicians and

Afrikaner business leaders, had begun its transition to a new South Africa with less resistance than Bloemfontein. Van der Walt agreed to visit and share what he had learnt. He made a compelling case in a rousing speech to students, despite some serious heckling. His presence helped soften attitudes, and the process of integration began.

The two young men – both of whom would graduate at the top of their respective disciplines – stayed in touch, their shared experience forging a lasting connection.

Both ended up in the South African capital Pretoria after their respective undergraduate studies. Van der Walt was completing his PhD in Artificial Intelligence (AI), regarded today as a recent phenomenon, but machine learning as a discipline was already in full swing and he was determined to be at the forefront of what he anticipated would be game-changing technology. Jonker was completing his articles at a firm in the city, and the pair would meet up at least every second weekend, light a fire for a braai (barbecue) and spend hours setting the world to rights. It became an unwritten rule that when they met up, the fire would be lit and eventually as the embers died down without so much as a thought about cooking, pizza would eventually be ordered.

While Jonker's upbringing had been nomadic, Van der Walt's was the opposite. He grew up and was schooled in Randfontein, a mining town to the west of Johannesburg, in a family steeped in business. His father, also named Tjaart, teamed up with another local entrepreneur, Sias du Toit, and the pair built a factory producing products that remain South African staples to this day: among them Nola mayonnaise and Bobtail pet food. The first image of a healthy-looking dog on the bag was of the family pet, a German Shepherd named Leeu – Afrikaans for 'Lion'. (As an aside, the Jonkers also had a dog called Leeu at one point – a bullmastiff.) Van der Walt senior was not about to pay an agency to find an appropriate canine to act as mascot for the brand when his own dog was perfectly good enough. Managing costs carefully was a key principle, which the younger Tjaart would harness through building his own enterprises later.

'We got business lessons at the dinner table from my dad all the time,' remembers Van der Walt. The most critical among them was the belief, based on his dealings with international suppliers of the expensive imported equipment he insisted on using in the factory, that South Africans were capable of competing anywhere. The second was that there was no such thing as a 'zero-sum game' – a situation where one party's gain was balanced by another's loss.

When Nola first hit the market, there was only one other brand of mayonnaise on South African shop shelves: Crosse & Blackwell. The owners at the time tried to dissuade the entrepreneurs from launching their brand, arguing it would be destructive for both parties. Instead, the category grew as mayonnaise was increasingly accepted by consumers as a condiment. It would be another valuable lesson when Tyme became the first new bank in 18 years to be awarded a licence in a market dominated by five retail incumbents.

'We would spend Sundays after church at the factory. It was exciting,' he recalls, remembering being influenced by generations of industrious figures. His maternal grandfather, Etienne Rousseau, was co-founder of the synthetic fuels business Sasol, which used the German-developed Fischer-Tropsch process to successfully extract oil from coal. South Africa faced crippling sanctions at the time. While it had no accessible oil reserves, coal was plentiful, and the government of the day knew it needed an alternative in its efforts to be self-sufficient in fuel production. 'It was an industrious, pioneering environment,' he says now.

Van der Walt would later join Sasol for 15 months straight out of university as a systems process engineer, but he was soon drawn to another state entity called the Foundation for Research Development (FRD), where he was made an executive director.

Like his lawyer friend, he was tasked with managing teams older and more experienced than he was. It proved to be a vital leadership lesson. Those professionals were unlikely to be responsive to being micro-managed by a recently graduated upstart, and he found it more effective to support talented people rather than begin issuing instructions. FRD became the country's largest research support agency during this period, primarily funding natural sciences and engineering. In 1999, it merged with the Centre for Science Development from the Human Sciences Research Council, leading to the formation of the National Research Foundation. Public funding in scientific research declined as the decade drew on and the private sector took up more of the slack.

While Jonker was building his legal career, Van der Walt was completing his PhD, developing mathematical tools to quantify data. He travelled extensively for the FRD, later establishing a national tech-focused venture capital fund framework informed by global lessons, and gained banking experience as a deputy general manager at The Business Bank before launching his own company, the venture capital firm Rock-IT.

The Business Bank, however, failed after it became entangled with Macmed, a healthcare group best remembered for its 'Easywee' product. It collapsed in one of South Africa's largest corporate fraud scandals at the time. Macmed had aggressively expanded using borrowed funds and, when its fraudulent activities came to light in 1999, the company went under, leaving creditors – including The Business Bank – exposed to massive losses. The bank was wound up, and its assets were sold off.

At 32, armed with some early scars and a small severance payout, Van der Walt teamed up with three university friends who were building a business called Crusader Systems, rooted in the data analytics they had studied at Stellenbosch. This led to the creation of a groundbreaking product, C-Sense, specialising in AI-driven data analytics. The team developed advanced machine-learning algorithms to streamline industrial processes and decision-making. Their work gained international recognition.

Crusader Systems was fast emerging as a serious player, reinforcing the idea that South Africa could produce globally competitive technology firms. In 2001, the company raised funding from friends and family, with Jonker participating in the first of many ventures where they would co-invest. When General Electric (GE) acquired the firm's technology assets in 2011 as part of its push into AI-powered industrial solutions for mining and heavy industry, integrating them into the GE Proficy Software Platform, the shareholders secured a significant payday – one that would later prove invaluable to the friends as their biggest shared project floundered at the edge of failure.

While Van der Walt built businesses, Jonker completed his MBA, and developed a passion for teaching, which he pursued part-time at GIBS. Jonker was also managing the law firm, which had become part of an ill-fated acquisition by Nedcor, the country's fourth largest banking group. He joined the financial services group's investment banking executive committee, which gave him a crash course in banking, consulting and regulation. Nedcor bought Edward Nathan in 1999, wanting to build an in-house corporate advisory business. The primary reason Nedbank bought the law firm is that it had separately listed its investment bank NIB. This meant it no longer had access to the corporate borrowers that Nedbank had, which had been a key source of investment banking deals. The logic was that by owning the law firm, they would get all Edward Nathan's transactions. The last thing the lawyers wanted, however, was to tie themselves to a single bank, so their interests were not as aligned as it was assumed they would be. The lawyers and bankers operated in silos, separated not just by a five-minute walk between buildings in Sandton, but by entirely different mindsets. When the deal was originally concluded, the world seemed to be moving in the direction of integrated advisory businesses combining law, corporate finance and change management into single firms. Soon after, however, a number of corporate failures, including Enron and Arthur Andersen, led to a swing away from integrated advisory to an emphasis on independence and the establishment of strong internal controls between the different disciplines. This structural change undermined the initial premise of the transaction and made it even more difficult to wring any synergies out of the Nedcor ownership of Edward Nathan.

Amid this, South Africa was hit by a banking crisis. It began with the collapse of Saambou Bank in 2002, triggering contagion that spread to BoE Bank, which Nedcor subsequently acquired. As panic set in among depositors, Nedcor itself became vulnerable. Only after Finance Minister Trevor Manuel, who had declined to intervene in Saambou Bank, stepped in to guarantee deposits did the panic subside. Not long after, Nedcor's controlling shareholder, Old Mutual, replaced the bank's leadership team, putting the former BoE CEO in charge. It was then that Jonker first met Tom Boardman.

Boardman took over as CEO of Nedcor at the end of 2002 and spent his first year conducting a comprehensive review of the bank's operations. One outcome of that review was his decision – negotiated with Jonker – to sell the law firm back to its partners at a loss. Boardman would later play a pivotal role in whether a buyer of last resort would step in to support a struggling Tyme Bank when its biggest shareholder was on the verge of shutting it down.

But we risk getting ahead of ourselves.

For now, the stage is set: two high-achieving friends, meeting regularly, co-investing in businesses and forging a deep bond grounded in mutual admiration. They came from vastly different backgrounds, but possessed complementary skill sets, values and ambition. They were also connected by an unwavering sense of loyalty and trust. Trust runs deep in this story, and over the next two decades.

It would be tested time and again.

Chapter 2

The Wrong Plus-One

It ought to be remembered that there is nothing more difficult to take in hand, more perilous to conduct, or more uncertain in its success, than to take the lead in the introduction of a new order of things. Because the innovator has for enemies all those who have done well under the old conditions, and lukewarm defenders in those who may do well under the new.
— Niccolò Machiavelli

If Coen Jonker's legal studies in Bloemfontein honed his expertise in law, and GIBS his understanding of business, it was Hernando de Soto's *The Mystery of Capital* that fundamentally shaped his sense of how social justice might be achieved.[1] It crystallised his belief that no amount of political contortion could begin to address the significant structural flaws at the foundation of one of the most economically polarised societies on earth. It was an access problem that needed a commercial solution.

He couldn't do that while running a powerful corporate law firm, so he gave notice, committing to Edward Nathan chairperson, Michael Katz, that he would extricate the firm from Nedcor and ensure it was on a steady footing before taking a sabbatical to ponder his next move. As it happened, the new Nedcor CEO, Tom Boardman, had promised shareholders he would divest of non-core assets and sold the law firm back to the partners for less than the bank had paid five years previously.

By the second half of 2005, Jonker was a free agent, but that didn't last long.

'In about October I got a call from my friend Johan Roets, who had recently joined Standard Bank. He said to me: "I hear you have lost your mind and given up the best job in law to think about financial inclusion. Standard Bank is employing interesting people, you need to meet the CEO,"' remembers Jonker.

In the second half of the 1990s South Africa's new government was getting antsy about including more people in the financial system and demanded banks find a solution to the problem or it would force them to do so. Standard Bank had been the most progressive of the Big Four groups in trying to solve the issue, and Jonker had a brief meeting with CEO Jacko Maree, who promptly handed him over to a rising star within the group named Sim Tshabalala. Like Jonker, Tshabalala had a law degree. He would later rise to the top job at Standard Bank and was eager for fresh thinking on the issue which, after several failed attempts, left the group stumped as to how it might proceed.

Its first serious attempt at providing financial services for poorer South Africans had been led by Bob Tucker, who had begun his career in banking as legal adviser to the Perm Building Society, colloquially referred to as 'The Perm', before being appointed as its managing director. Only building societies in those days provided residential mortgages. That was until the 1978 De Kock Commission recommended that banks, building societies, merchant banks and discount houses all be brought under one regulatory framework. This spelt an end to the building societies, which had enjoyed special tax benefits but lacked the capital base to survive under the new rules. That led to a round of industry consolidation, resulting in the creation of Absa and a range of other mergers.

Tucker had lobbied against the change, as he believed it would undermine the ability of black first-time homeowners to access finance. It was a lonely fight. His first effort to address the problem failed.

The Community Bank, which saw him team up with activist Ellen Kuzwayo and Cas Coovadia (who would later succeed him as head of the

Banking Association), also failed to gain traction.

Standard Bank recruited him to run Ebank, conceived as a standalone bank with its own distribution network, products and technology. It launched at the end of 1994, but it soon became apparent that it was too costly to have it operate independently of the bank. By the end of its first year, it had only 150,000 customers, so it was incorporated as a product rebranded E-Plan instead. The move made sense for the bank, as it allowed the offering to be enveloped by its existing infrastructure, and customer numbers picked up – an average of 70,000 a month opened accounts in the ten months to mid-1997. It was not alone in its efforts; Nedcor created its own standalone version aimed at low-income customers when it split The Perm into the Permanent Bank and People's Bank. It ran into the same cost and compliance issues, despite efforts to bolster it by folding FBC Fidelity Bank and NedEnterprise into the same vehicle. People's Bank was a top-ten institution in terms of assets, with a mission to focus on the underserved lower-income market, providing everything from instalment finance to loans and transactional banking. Like many others, including Saambou Bank and BoE Bank, it was a casualty of the 2001 small banks crisis, which resulted in another round of failures, consolidations and the emergence of a concentrated group of five major banks: Standard, FirstRand, Absa, Nedcor, Investec, plus a little startup called Capitec, which had its origins at this time as a consolidator of the rapacious informal lending sector. Capitec would later become the largest in terms of retail customers.

E-Plan users were encouraged to use what was at the time a highly evolved ATM network, which could not only take deposits, issue cash and carry out a range of transactions from balance checks to payments, but also printed cheques – obviating the need of customers in that segment to sign up for pricier checking accounts. As the 20th century ended, there were 1.4 million customers on E-Plan. The bank would have seen this as a success; however, it did not broaden financial inclusion to the extent that the country needed.

The biggest problem remained. More than 10 million people could still not afford to have a bank account or access a loan at a reasonable price point relative to their income. Independent research at the time established that only 27% of South Africans earning under R5,000 a month (equivalent to about US$700 at the time) had a bank account of any kind. Among those who did, only a few transacted several times a month. Most used the bank as a place to be paid before withdrawing their monthly salary in full in cash, rather than use the services on offer.

In 2003, Standard Bank tried again, this time in partnership with mobile phone operator MTN. There were plenty of synergies. Standard Bank was the biggest South African bank in Africa and MTN was growing its footprint across the continent and into the Middle East. Standard Bank understood banking, and MTN, by virtue of its expanding network, was reaching customers the bank could not.

MTN had poached marketing dynamo Santie Botha from Absa, where she had cemented the group's brand identity and had been the face of its innovative free internet service, in partnership with British IT company Affinity, as part of its drive to grow its consumer base and encourage its customers out of branches and to transact online.

Using her banking experience, Botha, now executive director of marketing at the mobile operator, proudly unveiled a joint venture with Standard Bank in 2005 called MTN Banking. It allowed its customers to perform financial transactions on their phones, including person-to-person payments, fund transfers and bill payments. It was revolutionary. Users could open accounts via software downloaded to their phones or pre-installed on SIM cards, with an additional digit added to their mobile number to create a unique account number. The system also offered a free SMS alert service to keep customers informed of their account activities. It was an idea ahead of its time. Neither the market nor the technology it needed were ready to deliver on a much-needed consumer proposition.

Regulators weren't satisfied with industry efforts, and banks, fearing regulation, collaborated to create the Mzansi account – a generic low-cost, low-feature, industry-wide offering that they could plug into their systems. It was based on a magnetic stripe debit card platform and was launched by the Big Four banks – Standard Bank, FirstRand, Absa and Nedcor – together with the state-owned Postbank, in October 2004.

Clearly, there was a need for a product. Six million accounts were opened in four years – 90% of them were first-time account holders. According to the South African Reserve Bank, the number of people over 16 with an account increased from fewer than half to nearly two-thirds, or some 20 million people, by 2008.[2] That initial success was eclipsed by the reality that the product was unappealing to the segment it was meant to serve. Within months of opening, half the accounts were inactive and the bank balances they held were a fraction of those in comparable commercial accounts: US$28 vs US$191, with half the number of monthly transactions.

A 2009 report commissioned by Finmark Trust found the early success of Mzansi account sign-ups 'reflected the pent-up demand for accessible, affordable, safe places to transact and store value'.[3] On the other hand, the report noted, because Mzansi was conceived as a collaborative response to the threat of government intervention, rather than as a means of pursuing a commercial opportunity, it demonstrated the complexity of large, multi-product, multi-segment banks accessing that segment of the market. The report concluded that the participating banks quickly gained market knowledge and experience that they did not have before and may not have otherwise obtained.

The standout feature of Mzansi was that Capitec had declined the invitation to participate in the programme. It opted instead to develop offerings the market wanted. That strategy was part of its success and would eventually make it the biggest retail bank in South Africa, with more than 22 million customers serviced by 850 branches.

While M-Pesa in Kenya had thrived because there were no alternatives, South Africa's well-developed financial services market was evolving at an unprecedented pace. The upstart online-only bank 20Twenty had demonstrated the capabilities of branchless digital banking. While it ultimately failed because of poor partnerships, first with Saambou Bank and later with Standard Chartered, it forced established banks to up their electronic offerings.

It was in this environment that Jonker set about turning the theory he had been teaching at GIBS into practice, using the best learnings from the likes of M-Pesa to Bangladesh's Grameen Bank, and the highly successful Bank Rakyat Indonesia, which focused on microfinance via a substantial network across the country, lending to small businesses and rural communities.

Tucker was back at Standard Bank following his time at the Banking Association, and he and Jonker created a new offering they called Community Banking, reporting to Tshabalala. Aware of the limitations of Tucker's previous efforts, the idea was to build a business model independent of the constraints of the strict governance, compliance and costs that had hampered previous efforts.

To achieve that, it needed to operate under the radar. They developed a 'skunkworks' inside the bank. Skunkworks is a term that originated within Lockheed Martin's Advanced Development Programs, which was responsible for a number of highly classified research and development programmes. In the case of Community Banking, it was more an experimental laboratory, independent of outside influence. Most people in the bank were oblivious to its existence and, as it was housed under different divisions and different executives at different times, it was difficult to track.

'We were left to our own devices, and within 24 months we got scale with more than 1 million people signed up in communities via mobile agents who could immediately issue a customer with a debit card from a blister pack. We did some experimental lending using corporate social investment money, rather than putting the loans onto the bank balance sheet,' says Jonker.

They set about breaking almost every rule the bank held dear, which was fine, until it wasn't. They had identified more than half a dozen key rural communities they called 'the magnificent 7', where the bank had no presence and there was potential to sign up customers. Android technology was only commercially available on smartphones from September 2008, so the team had to use the best it had available at the time. They hired teams of roaming agents armed with BlackBerry phones to sign up clients, whose pictures they snapped using a Sony Cybershot digital camera. Once their applications were manually approved via a complex back-office process, they were able to deposit and withdraw cash via point-of-sale devices in privately owned local shops, known colloquially as spaza stores.

'It was phenomenally successful,' recalls Dominique Collett, who had stumbled across Community Banking while working on projects for group financial director Simon Ridley. 'When I told him I wanted to join Coen's team, he asked: "Are you mad?"' Collett was fascinated by the drive to provide financial solutions at a low cost, but it does suggest that there was some scepticism among senior executives that a motley assortment of maverick bankers, lawyers, activists, thinkers, theorists and academics, united by the goal of making banking accessible, could do it.

One member of that 'motley crew' was Thoraya Pandy, a journalist who had been a senior official in the National Treasury, working for Finance Minister Trevor Manuel and Director General Maria Ramos, before joining the bank. Her time in the public sector heightened her appreciation of what Jonker was seeking to address. 'I immediately fell in love with the vision of driving financial inclusion, while making it commercially viable. Coenraad had a formidable commitment to making it work – he had no idea what a stop sign was.'

The pace and pressure of experimentation were relentless. 'Those guys were crazy,' recalls a senior Standard Bank executive. 'They didn't play by the same rules as the rest of the bank.' The reality was that Community Banking was an anathema, and even though it was signing up new customers at a faster rate than any other part of the business – up to 7,000 a day – its approach scared the establishment.

'They brought daily innovation and a great understanding of the market, especially low-income and spaza shops. They knew that market very well,' acknowledges Tshabalala. 'They challenged our hierarchy and formality, which the textbooks will tell you is fantastic, but it just does not work in rules-driven, process-driven institutions, and I suspect that is why these innovations inside financial institutions always fail, because they go against the compliance-driven, rules-based approach that big financial institutions need, which makes it very, very hard for innovators.'

The fact that it was built on the same platform that had been used to create the MTN Banking joint venture before it, and not on the Standard

Bank mainframe, meant it remained largely invisible to the compliance and marketing departments. It thrived precisely because no one really appreciated what they were up to. That was fine if it was a skunkworks, but it was never going to fly when subjected to the microscopic rigours the rest of the bank was obliged to operate under.

John Kane was recruited onto the team by a guest lecturer during his MBA. He wanted to learn something new and escape the filth of industrial parks where he was working at the time. He had an Arts degree in Philosophy and Psychology and had been working in the packaging industry for a decade. He discovered after university that he loved making dull processes efficient. Part of his job was to ensure cost-effective replicability in a low-margin business.

He had written a paper on the shortcomings of systems implementations through a failure to understand process outcomes. 'I don't really remember the contents, but it obviously struck a chord. I was brought in as implementation manager, with the brief to take Community Banking from an idea to reality quickly by using process and technology.' Kane's first job was to run parts of the project that benefited from his thinking, which supported the idea of driving a high-volume business with low costs. He was working on the Sony Cybershot process, as well as the management and distribution of cards and the Know Your Customer (KYC) system, which allowed customers to be verified and supported by call-centre agents, who were kept busy by the volume of new clients.

'We fell afoul of the bank's systems several times. You still needed cards in the Standard Bank system, and we often unintentionally broke things because the pace and manner of our growth were not catered for in the existing systems. As such, we did things like add 100,000 cards to a single branch, while it had been hard-coded a decade before that no branch could have more than a fixed number of cards – it was something random like 86,767,' says Kane. The incident did not endear the team to the Standard Bank bosses. No one in the group was able to load new cards, and it took 'some time' to figure out why. 'That didn't engender the idea of us being left alone to our own devices, much longer.'

It was surprising they got as far as they did before there was an inevitable corporate intervention. It might have continued for longer had Community Banking not achieved the scale and impact it did, which inevitably and increasingly affected other parts of the bank.

'It became clear that you couldn't run a cult on the side of the bank,' says Tshabalala.

Before long, like Ebank before it, Community Banking was brought back under the control of the bank, which meant it would have to run off the costly core SAP platform, be subjected to the more rigorous governance and risk frameworks under which the bank functioned, and would have central costs allocated to it, which again pushed up the pricing. It would also not be able to differentiate from a brand perspective, as the group had decided it should operate under one banner, doing away with icons like the investment bank SCMB and Stannic, the asset finance business, and, as it turned out, Community Banking.

The clock started ticking on Jonker's time at Standard Bank when he lost his autonomy and was instructed to report to a senior executive, with a view to integrate it into the labyrinthian group structure. 'The moment these customers walked into a branch, they were unprofitable,' says Jonker. What made sense for the bank did not make sense for the mission he and his team had embarked upon.

With the benefit of hindsight, the offering was doomed before it even began. While the Community Banking team was playing to win, the group was playing to not lose. Jonker had spent more than five years at Standard Bank, and his project had gone the way of its predecessors.

However, Jonker's enthusiasm for what needed to be built was undiminished. If anything, it strengthened his resolve. Critical relationships had been forged and vital lessons learnt at someone else's expense. The biggest of these was that the last place to develop a banking disruptor was inside a bank. It needed to be independent, but how do you fund an idea?

Pandy suggests that if Jonker was not a banker, he might have been a spiritual leader of some description. People were inclined to follow him, many giving up established roles in large companies to rally around the vision he created. Jonker blushes at the description, preferring to portray his persuasive powers as having the ability to tell stories about something that does not yet exist and doing it in a way that mobilises others to bring it to fruition.

'We spoke this business into existence,' says Tauriq Keraan, who at the time was representing Deloitte Consulting and doing project work in the bank under an ambitious growth-orientated CEO named Louis Geeringh. Both were enthralled by what Jonker was looking to achieve and shared his mounting frustration at the inflexibility of Standard Bank, as Community Banking was passed from executive to executive, who handled it like a ticking time bomb, eager to pass it on before it exploded in their hands.

So Geeringh and Jonker hatched a plan. Jonker would leave the bank and join Deloitte Consulting as a partner, with little more than a 'let's see what we can do together' promise.

'Standard Bank had spent hundreds of millions of rands on what was ultimately a futile endeavour,' maintains Geeringh, still frustrated by the fact that large companies routinely failed to grasp the potential of servicing the mass market. 'This is a story of missed opportunity by many, many, many large corporates in South Africa and internationally that had the opportunity to have Tyme, but because of bureaucracy, internal governance, indecision and in some cases uselessness, were just never able to capitalise on the vision of what Tyme is today.'

For Jonker, and key members of the team who would follow him to Deloitte, the time spent at Standard Bank was invaluable. It had allowed for a period of unfettered experimentation and, most importantly, a place for a core team to coalesce.

They knew what didn't work. Now they needed to figure out what would.

Part II

The Ideas That Shaped Tyme

Chapter 3

From Branches to Backends

*The greatest danger in times of turbulence is not the turbulence –
it is to act with yesterday's logic.*
— Peter Drucker

Breaking the bank

Tyme Group, in its current form, first went to market with the South African-based digital bank, TymeBank. It was 2019 when the business launched under the first new banking licence the South African Reserve Bank had issued in nearly two decades. In and of itself, this was a notable feat. However, more than this, the bank was awarded the licence on the back of having convinced the regulator that TymeBank would operate digitally, in the cloud.

While in one sense this was a significant first in the South African setting, the retail bank was born into an industry that was changing rapidly around the world.

To make sense of the changes afoot, consider other industries that have been through rapid transformation. How many cars should a taxi service own? The more the better, we once assumed. Uber, DiDi, Grab, Gojek, Lyft and Yandex have shattered that paradigm. How much land should a hotelier own? None, according to Airbnb, Booking.com and Expedia. Our 'truths' are being upended to the extent that dynamism is the new status quo. In this environment, there are no sacred cows. To thrive at the tumultuous coalface of this rapidly changing world, businesses need the courage and creativity to question everything. Banking – by which we mean retail banking – is no exception.

Gradually, then suddenly: How digital banking is rewriting the rules

What is a bank? Perhaps as recently as a decade ago, the answer was straightforward. Additionally, we had a strong understanding of the drivers that propelled traditional banks to dominance, including geography and economic footprint; industrialisation and urbanisation; and an extensive (read expensive) network of branches. In 2012, when Jonker first suggested the idea of building a standalone bank with no branches, no ATMs, no middle office, and no paper or physical cash anywhere in the system, an experienced retail banker responded, 'Then what you are building is not a bank.'

Today a new trio – globalisation, scalable digital business models and rapid customer adoption – is driving retail banking, reshaping how banks operate and redefining who leads the pack. The convergence of these forces supports the suggestion that in the next ten years, the world's biggest retail banks might be digital banks, displacing the traditional bank that we came to know and trust so well.

China's WeBank has already stolen a march on this prediction. It is the world's largest digital bank and the largest bank overall by customer count. WeBank serves 320 million individuals and 2.7 million micro-, small- and medium-sized enterprises (MSMEs). Founded in 2014, WeBank leverages advanced blockchain technology to handle high transaction volumes with remarkable efficiency. Averaging 2.8 million new customers each month, it far outpaces competitors in customer acquisition and operational scale. WeBank is twice the size of the world's next biggest bank by customer count, Banco Santander, which was founded in 1857 and has about 165 million customers.

Without doubt, there is a growing strain on old banking models, ominous of impending collapse and replacement, or at the very least, material displacement of the incumbents.

Consider another compelling case that helps make this point. Until recently, measured by number of customers, Brazil's Itaú Unibanco was the largest retail bank in Latin America. Almost a century old, the bank serves approximately 70 million clients globally. By comparison, Nubank, the digital bank founded in Brazil in 2013, had a customer count of 75 million by 2022; 85 million customers by 2023; and at the end of 2024 announced that its customer base had hit 110 million.[1]

Nubank doesn't have a single branch in its three countries of operation, Brazil, Colombia and Mexico. Itaú Unibanco has 4,335 branches in Brazil alone. Make no mistake, the incumbent is still in fine form, but its decades of dominance have been displaced. And quickly. In December 2024 Nubank spread its wings beyond Latin America by investing in Tyme. But more about this in Chapter 14.

With 1.7 billion people globally unbanked – or about a quarter of the world's bankable population – digital banking's expansion is timely.[2] Digital banks excel in accessibility, speed and efficiency. TymeBank in South Africa has been an industry leader in this regard. Customers are onboarded in under five minutes; no branch visit is required. The entire process is paperless, and the customer acquisition cost is about US$5 per customer, compared to US$30 per customer for its nearest competitor and above US$100 per customer among the industry's established banks.

As digital replaces physical in more and more spheres of life, these examples begin to look less like outliers and start to resemble an industrial-scale tidal wave. Pontsho Ramontsha, communications manager at TymeBank, gives early evidence of Tyme's impact: 80,000 customers signed up in the first month after launch, and within nine months the bank onboarded 1 million customers. By the middle of 2022, and in under three years since launch, TymeBank had onboarded 5 million customers. By 2023, Ramontsha reports, one in every five eligible (16 years and older) South Africans had a TymeBank account, amounting to a total of 8 million customers, with 200,000 new customers still being added each month. At the time of writing, TymeBank is the country's third largest bank by customers.

But the sceptic may retort that the big, traditional banks are still in charge. They still have their names on skyscrapers. Well, old dogs are learning new tricks. Traditional banks are digitising as fast as they can. And the ones that do it faster perform better.

Growth, gravity and the great escape

Across markets, industries and time, the macroeconomy is the strongest gravitational force acting on business performance. The size and health of a country's economy are the single biggest drivers of firm performance, shaping both revenues and returns.

Eighty years of US data show a near linear relationship between the size of the economy and private sector profits.[3] The same holds globally. The performance of the MSCI All Country World Index shows that economic growth is the single biggest driver of revenue and earnings for the world's 2,900 largest firms. In banking, the effect is especially visible. The world's largest banks by Tier 1 capital over the last half-century mirror the rise and fall of national economies: US banks dominated in the 1970s, Japan overtook them in the 1980s, then European and US banks re-emerged to take up the reins in the 1990s, and Chinese banks now hold top spots.

Seen through this lens, TymeBank's success in South Africa – a country that has seen over a decade of economic stagnation – looks like an act of defiance. Per capita incomes are lower today than they were 15 years ago, yet Tyme has grown rapidly by serving customers neglected by the traditional system. That alone should raise eyebrows.

But there is more going on here than a statistical outlier. Tyme's success in South Africa – despite a sluggish economy and stagnant per capita incomes – points to a deeper shift. The historically tight link between economic growth and firm performance is loosening. Globalisation, scalable digital business models and rapid consumer adoption are redrawing the map for modern banking. These dynamics do not eliminate economic gravity, but they do offer a way to escape it. And in Tyme's case, they help explain how a digital bank can scale across markets, leapfrog incumbents and build momentum even in the toughest conditions. And you will find these three forces at the heart of nearly every conversation with Tyme's founders, executives and strategists – because they are the scaffolding on which the group's growth has been built.

Globalisation: Leaving boundaries behind

The first force driving the shape of the banking industry and facilitating Tyme Group's drive, globalisation, has been thoroughly analysed. But that does not mean it is a waning force. Steven Altman and Caroline Bastian highlight this in the *DHL Global Connectedness Report 2024*. Using Pankaj Ghemawat's four pillars of trade, capital, information and people (TCIP) to measure global connectedness,[4] Altman and Bastian show that globalisation reached a record high in 2022 and remained close to that level in 2023.[5]

This ascent in globalisation bounds ahead, despite shocks and setbacks like the 2007/2008 financial crisis and the Covid-19 pandemic. Notably, while the setback of global lockdown collapsed the movement of people and dramatically constrained flows of trade and capital, information dynamics were free to keep growing. In fact, the shock strengthened information flows by spurring greater investment in information technology and enduringly altering our habits.

Nate Clarke, CEO of GoTyme in the Philippines, highlights the significance of this moment for Tyme. The pandemic served as a windfall for digital banking in countries where cash had long dominated everyday transactions. Practically overnight, the economy was forced to go digital, as lockdowns and mobility restrictions made in-person interactions impractical or impossible.

The Bangko Sentral ng Pilipinas (BSP), the country's central bank, responded by accelerating its push for digital adoption, while platforms like GCash and PayMaya saw rapid growth. Digital wallets became essential, QR codes replaced cash at even the smallest retailers, and millions of Filipinos entered the formal financial system – many for the first time. Today, GoTyme is the fastest-growing bank in the country, with Covid-induced digital adoption as a critical enabler of its momentum.

PART II: THE IDEAS THAT SHAPED TYME

The power of platforms

The second force at play is the phenomenon of the platform business model. Businesses leveraging this create value by facilitating exchanges or interactions between two or more interdependent groups, typically producers and consumers.[6] The superpower of platform businesses is scalability: they leverage network effects, where increased participation enhances the value of the platform, leading to exponential growth potential with relatively low marginal costs as user numbers grow.

This is evident in Tyme Group's model, where, between mid-2019 and the end of 2024, TymeBank's customer base grew from 200,000 to 9.7 million – an increase of almost 50 times. Yet, operating expenses grew from US$17 million in the third quarter of 2019 to US$23 million in the fourth quarter of 2024 – an increase of just 0.3 times. This shows the exceptional leverage in the business model that allows a company like TymeBank to scale rapidly compared to traditional businesses.

Although we treat platform businesses as synonymous with digital varieties, it is worth remembering that platforms can be physical.

An iconic example of a physical business that has scaled impressively is 60-year-old Walmart, which has 10,586 locations, selling over 75 million items in 19 different countries. From this example, it is evident that scaling with platform-like dynamics is not monopolised by digital businesses. However, while Walmart's scale is impressive, its model is inherently constrained by physical bounds. And it is for this reason that the business – and many other firms facing similar constraints – has pivoted in recent years to embrace a digital model by building a so-called phygital business. This proposition blends physical and digital options, allowing customers to choose their preferred interaction method, while receiving consistent service across all touch points.

While Walmart morphed into this mixed approach from a fully physical foundation, Tyme Group's digital-first way incorporated the physical dimension to support and supplement their online roots. We explain the ingenuity of Tyme's phygitisation through kiosks later.

However, no traditional business has come close to achieving the scale, speed of growth and reach that the likes of Uber, Airbnb and LinkedIn can boast with digital platforms. Consider Alibaba's story. Since its inception in 2003, Alibaba's online marketplace, Taobao, has grown to host over 1 billion product listings across 220 countries and territories.[7]

The same pattern plays out across emerging markets. MercadoLibre, often called the 'Amazon of Latin America', operates in 18 countries and has over 148 million active users, with a logistics and fintech arm that reaches deeper than most banks.

In India, Jio Platforms, a digital ecosystem built around mobile data, gained over 400 million users in under five years, reshaping mobile access, payments and entertainment. Gojek in Indonesia began as a ride-hailing app, but scaled into a digital super-app offering everything from payments to food delivery to telehealth – processing millions of daily transactions across Southeast Asia. In Nigeria, Flutterwave, a digital payments company, now connects over 30 countries and processes billions in annual transactions, enabling cross-border trade for African MSMEs.

Digital models scale much quicker and with far greater reach than physical models. Increasingly, they define the new infrastructure of emerging and advanced market economies.[8]

Digital platforms also enable a blank-sheet approach. Airbnb affords a good example. Prior to its arrival, we all assumed that growth for an accommodation business meant building more rooms and filling them more frequently. Airbnb showed that a tourist accommodation business doesn't need to own a single room.

Tyme's take on platform strategy is interesting in that, like Airbnb, it spans the digital and physical worlds. In addition to being able to engage with the bank purely through an app, customers also have access to a network of kiosks, brand ambassadors and the checkout counters of retail partners for cash management. On this score, Ramontsha notes that Tyme has 1,650 kiosks deployed at retail stores, with 1,000 in South Africa and 650 in the Philippines. In addition to these kiosks, she says, 'Our phygital model also incorporates retail checkout points for cash withdrawals and deposits, with approximately 200,000 points available in South Africa through retail partnerships.' These physical touch points effectively replicate the sales, service and cash management functions of traditional bank branches, but at a fraction of the cost. By leveraging the existing infrastructure of retailers, Tyme goes some way towards giving its customers the best of two worlds, without owning a single branch.

Ramontsha also emphasises that Tyme's impact extends well beyond its customer base. In partnership with Harambee, a youth employment accelerator, TymeBank has created meaningful job opportunities for young South Africans who were previously unemployed. These youth have formed a vital part of TymeBank's front-line sales force, playing a significant role in driving the bank's rapid customer growth. A key principle of the programme was to hire locally, and young people were recruited from the communities where kiosks were located. This approach had two major benefits: it ensured that TymeBank ambassadors were serving their own communities, and it eliminated high transport costs that often act as a barrier to employment. As a rule, no ambassador should have to take more than one taxi ride to get to work. To date, more than 5,500 young people have been employed through this partnership, turning TymeBank kiosks into both financial access points and engines of inclusive economic participation.

The principle can be generalised across industries. With an app and a brand, new models can topple old ones – no matter how obvious the established approach may be. No one has immunity to disruption.

Consumer adoption: Ready, steady, go

An insatiable consumer readiness to embrace new businesses doing new things – or old things in new ways – completes a powerful trifecta of industrial disruption. And this sits at the heart of the Tyme Group's strategy. Unless individuals trust, want and like new technologies and products, the case for hyper-scaling via the cloud is academic.

Using historical adoption curves, Citi Digital strategy shows that the telephone, radio and television took 75 years, 38 years and 13 years, respectively, to reach 50 million users. In contrast, more recent innovations achieved this milestone at a much faster pace. The internet reached 50 million users in four years. ChatGPT took a month. Meta's Threads slashed that to one day.[9]

The upshot is that consumers are ready and willing to move from concrete to cloud if it means meeting a need better. And globalisation and technological innovation have condensed the time frames for mass adoption across different industries.[10]

There is an important caveat. While digital models enable rapid scaling and global reach, they often operate in 'winner-takes-all' or 'winner-takes-most' markets. The 2025 'State of Subscription Apps', sampling 75,000 apps, demonstrates this sharply: the top 5% of newly launched apps earn over 400 times more in their first two years than the bottom 25%, and just 19% ever reach US$1,000 in monthly recurring revenue.[11]

Beyond that, the drop-off is steep. While apps are just part of a digital system – and only partly represent digital banks – the findings show that while digital platforms offer immense opportunity, the spoils go to the champions. As Ricky Bobby quips in *Talladega Nights*, 'If you ain't first, you're last.'[12] It is a blunt mantra, but it captures a hard truth: in today's hyper-competitive environment, second place often feels like failure.

Tyme's challenge is cut out. Its multi-market presence and rapid scale-up – especially in markets as competitive as South Africa and the Philippines – certainly show champion DNA. In an environment where scale is possible but far from guaranteed, there is no room to rest on laurels.

The power of precision: Why contextual finance is leaving embedded models behind

Achieving critical mass is one thing. But building a business – any business – at scale does not automatically make the business a force for good. What matters is intention, context and design.

The Tyme Group's banks find their edge not merely in technology or convenience, but in something more profound: embedding themselves in the context of people's lives, aspirations and communities. By doing so, they move from being simply functional to becoming transformative. As

PART II: THE IDEAS THAT SHAPED TYME

Louis Geeringh, co-founder of Futureworld and former global strategy lead at Deloitte, observes: 'Equity value doesn't drive Coen [Jonker]; it is the purpose of bringing dignity to people and giving them financial inclusion.' That sense of purpose – of enabling financial participation and restoring dignity – is what ultimately sets Tyme apart.

This philosophy of 'meeting customers where they are' is evident not just in rhetoric, but in action, says Ramontsha. A recent example is TymeBank's partnerships with Kazang and Flash, two of South Africa's leading payment solution providers. These partnerships dramatically extend the bank's physical reach by turning informal retail outlets into full-service banking points.

Through its collaboration with Flash, TymeBank customers can now withdraw cash at over 172,000 spaza shops and traders across South Africa. This gives TymeBank the widest cash-withdrawal footprint in the country. Similarly, the partnership with Kazang enables customers to use their TymeBank cards to withdraw cash at tens of thousands of Kazang Pay-enabled outlets. These informal traders – long central to community commerce – are now equipped to offer far more than groceries. Customers can buy prepaid electricity, airtime, data and gaming vouchers, pay bills, send remittances and access cash – all from a single, trusted location.

Kazang itself operates a national network of over 90,000 value-added services devices, processing about 3 million transactions daily, with 60,000 of these now capable of card acceptance and cash withdrawals through its Kazang Pay platform for micro-merchants. Cheslyn Jacobs, TymeBank's chief commercial officer, comments, 'Among our 11 million customers are many who still rely heavily on physical cash for day-to-day transactions. By working with Kazang, we can offer them more points where they can access easy withdrawals at shops and traders that are not only accessible but embedded within their communities.'

This approach – bringing financial services into everyday environments through community-based infrastructure – is not just operationally smart; it reflects deeper shifts in how finance is being reimagined. Tyme's model illustrates the real-world application of what scholars and strategists have come to describe as contextual finance: banking that disappears into the background of daily life, while becoming more impactful.

For Tyme, this means building a financial ecosystem that does not simply provide access, but creates meaningful pathways for empowerment and upward mobility, embedding financial services seamlessly into the lives of users through intuitive onboarding and real-time credit decisions that recognise responsible behaviour. Tyme aspires to do more than just scale; it seeks to create value that resonates deeply with the people it serves.

At Tyme, that purpose runs through the very structure of the services it delivers, eliminating banking fees to improve household savings; using behavioural nudges to reward clients with higher returns on their deposits; and offering merchant loans without a single piece of paper. All these serve as working examples of contextual finance in action.

Jonker believes that contextual banking is the future. So much so that customer satisfaction measured by net promoter scores (NPS) is among the most important metrics to assess the Tyme banks' performances. Ranging between +100 to −100, NPS provides a simple yet powerful way to measure customer loyalty, pain points, benchmarking against competitors and areas impacting growth, and for identifying areas of improvement. Customers near +100 love the company and become evangelists. Those near −100 are furious about something and will tell everyone they can.

GoTyme executive Raymund Villanueva talks about the way evangelists enable scale. 'Scaling from 0 to 5 million customers requires specific startup skills, "Bob the Builders". Getting from 5 to 15 million customers requires "Sam the Scalers". Brand building is not about marketing, it's about the product and user experience – delight one, win ten.'

To explain why NPS matters so much to the banks, Jonker gives two practical examples.

The first example is Tyme's product called merchant cash advance, which offers working-capital finance for small businesses. Jonker explains: 'If your business has a point-of-sale device, we analyse your payment data and offer you a loan based on what that tells us. There are no forms to fill out, no bank managers you need to impress. And there are no monthly repayments;

instead, we take a percentage of turnover to repay the loan. You never have to hand over money you don't have. If you have a bad month, you pay less. This is a model that just works – for us and for our users. Our NPS on merchant cash advance is over 80. If you are familiar with the NPS metric, you'll know that's stratospheric.'

The second example is that customarily painful process of opening a bank account. Traditionally, to open an account with a new bank, customers would go to a branch, stand in a queue, hand over the requisite documents, wait while data is captured, and maybe 45 minutes later (not considering travel time) they would have a new account. Often a second visit would be required to collect a debit card. And the account would only be active the next day. In comparison, TymeBank can open a fully compliant account in less than five minutes. And customers can do it from their living room. And the account is active immediately.

This is simply a better way of banking in the modern context. It is not that we like to do these things on our phones – it is just how we live our lives. Digital banks are meeting us in our context.

Frontier country

Nobody ever said it was easy living in frontier country. Change, quite simply, hurts.

From his position at Deloitte, Geeringh saw the Tyme story unfold with a mix of admiration and frustration. 'Tyme is a story of missed opportunity by many large corporates,' he says, reflecting on how close some incumbents came to building what Tyme ultimately became. One bank, he recalls, had the chance to birth the equivalent of TymeBank in South Africa – but never managed to get out of its own way. 'It's trapped in a fossilised structure,' Geeringh explains, 'carrying R20 billion in coding on the balance sheet. That sunk cost has to be amortised across old and new clients alike. And for that bank, it makes real innovation almost impossible.'

But it is not just banks that offend Geeringh. The telco giant MTN, too, failed to absorb TymeBank and its revolutionary business model. In commenting on the attempted acquisition, he recalls, 'The corporate antibody response was swift. They needed Tyme on premises and on payroll within weeks. But that kind of agility just wasn't possible inside MTN's machinery.' In Geeringh's telling, the pattern was clear: opportunity presented itself, but the host rejected the transplant. This makes it much harder for the incumbents – whether banks, or telcos leaning into finance or some other large corporate for that matter – to jump tracks. Tjaart van der Walt agrees. He notes, 'Because of this mindset, a successful "absorption" of the Tyme project by MTN would most likely have resulted in yet another failed attempt to build a disruptor – much like what happened with Standard Bank.' But more about this part of our story in Chapter 6.

Digital banking is not just an alternative way of doing business; it is a completely different paradigm. Guilherme Lago, the chief financial officer (CFO) of Nubank, describes the shift as a textbook case of industrial disruption, where banks can serve more people, offer a better experience, charge less and still deliver strong unit economics. That is not just digital – it is architectural. Yet incumbents remain convinced that their way is the only way. They cannot fathom that a bank without physical infrastructure, legacy overheads or geographic constraints might not just be viable, but superior. And by the time they do, it may already be too late.

The future of banking: A new world order

David Vélez, co-founder and chief executive officer of Brazil's Nubank, quipped: 'First they ignore you, then they laugh at you, then they fight you, then you win.'[13] Vélez's remark echoes a deeper historical truth about how radical shifts – whether in business, science or society – are initially dismissed, then fiercely resisted, before becoming self-evident.

What applies to scientific revolutions also applies to business: truly disruptive companies – whether Nubank, Tyme or the digital banking model itself – must pass through this gauntlet before achieving legitimacy.

The model of low-cost acquisition, paperless onboarding and contextualised financial services across emerging markets are not only viable, but also quietly reconstituting the idea of what a bank can be. In this sense, Tyme is not only participating in the digital-first revolution – it is helping define it.

On this point, the digital-first revolution has shown what banks need not be. Just like hotel chains no longer need rooms, banks don't need branches. Traditional banks, once dominant by virtue of geography, limited competition and high barriers to entry created by branch networks, are highly vulnerable to digital challengers whose models thrive on agility, efficiency and customer-centric innovation, and whose reach is fed by globalisation and enabled by the cloud.

In a world where platforms proliferate and consumers readily adopt new technologies – where the benefits of banking are transformative for individual clients and broader communities – digital banks, unshackled by legacy systems and unnecessary overheads, have the brightest, most scalable futures.

Chapter 4

Hidden in Plain Sight

A well-functioning financial system is not an end in itself, but a means to an end: inclusive and sustainable growth.
— Joseph Stiglitz

Banks matter. They are indispensable institutions that perform a multitude of vital functions: mobilising savings, allocating credit, managing risk and promoting financial inclusion. Historical evidence, theoretical models and empirical studies converge on the same conclusion: well-functioning banking systems are essential for stimulating economic growth, reducing poverty and ensuring financial stability. As societies confront growing challenges, such as income inequality, technological disruption and financial volatility, the role of banks remains central in fostering environments where individuals and businesses can thrive.

More than 1.7 billion people worldwide remain unbanked or underbanked – locked out of the financial systems that enable wealth accumulation, insurance against risk, firm productivity and broader economic growth. Digital banking, with its capacity to leapfrog physical infrastructure and reduce cost to serve, could be to financial inclusion what antibiotics were to infection or what vaccines were to polio: a scalable, transformative remedy.

Two constants: Change and trust
If death and taxes are the only guarantees in life, the banking equivalent

might well be that models change constantly, but trust is the universal constant of the financial world. Throughout history, banks that have upheld the values of integrity, transparency and accountability have flourished.[1] The Medici Bank, for example, rose to prominence in Renaissance Italy by earning and maintaining the trust of its clients. In contrast, the collapse of Lehman Brothers in 2008 stands as a cautionary tale of what happens when trust is breached.[2]

In the digital era, trust is more important and more fragile than ever. Fintech innovation and digital-first banking have opened unprecedented opportunities for access and efficiency – but they also bring heightened risks around cybersecurity, data privacy and algorithmic bias.[3] In an era of heightened scrutiny and empowered consumers, trust must be earned and preserved through robust regulatory compliance, ethical practice, and transparent, customer-centric communication. As banks transcend borders and become increasingly embedded in the digital fabric of everyday life, preserving trust is no longer a one-time achievement – it is a continuous effort.

In fact, in our conversations with Tyme, one word surfaced as frequently as 'technology': 'trust', and that trust is as foundational to banking as capital itself. For a digital bank operating without branches, across geographies and often among first-time banking customers, trust isn't a given – it must be carefully established and constantly curated.

The potential impact of banks
Whether delivered in person or through pixels, banks impact nearly every aspect of our financial lives. That is, for those with access. Until recently, access to banking was largely determined by the ability to physically enter a branch. In the 1990s, access became a hybrid of bricks and bandwidth. Today, we are in the foothills of a new era – the age of digital-first banking, which promises to remove the final barriers to financial inclusion. A savings account can be the gateway to resilience, opportunity and upward mobility: paying school fees, starting a small business or withstanding a financial shock. And now all the trust, resilience and utility traditionally associated

with banking institutions can be delivered through a mobile phone – only faster, cheaper and more scalable than ever before. And Tyme is a driving force in this global transition.

The ongoing evolution of the banking sector – driven by innovation, regulatory reforms, and a broad social and political commitment to achieve economic and financial inclusion – promises to enhance the sector's contributions to economic well-being and development in the future. Policymakers, financial institutions and researchers must continue to collaborate to harness the full potential of banks in promoting sustainable growth and social progress. Ultimately, the success of modern economies depends on the ability of banks to adapt, innovate and provide critical financial services that empower communities and drive prosperity worldwide.

The life's work of two sublime thinkers can be harnessed to provide a framework to think through the importance of banking – not just for some, but as a rising tide for us all. First, consider C.K. Prahalad. The professor from the University of Michigan makes his case in *The Fortune at the Bottom of the Pyramid: Eradicating Poverty through Profits*.[4] He challenges the traditional notion that serving low-income populations – the 'poor' – is primarily a charitable endeavour. Instead, he posits that the poorest segments of society represent a significant and largely untapped market opportunity.

According to Prahalad, businesses that innovate to meet the unique needs of these consumers can simultaneously drive profit and foster social inclusion. By designing affordable products and services that resonate with the bottom of the pyramid, companies not only expand their market reach but also contribute to economic empowerment and poverty reduction. As Prahalad explains with characteristic clarity, 'The future lies with those companies who see the [excluded] as their customers. Strategy is about stretching limited resources to fit ambitious aspirations. If your aspirations are not greater than your resources, you're not an entrepreneur.'

It will come as no surprise that Prahalad had a profound influence in shaping Jonker and Van der Walt's thoughts and beliefs and helping them formulate the principles that underpin Tyme. It is difficult to get too far into a conversation about the purpose of their business without Prahalad being referenced in the conversation.

Our second banking brain is Hernando de Soto, whose best-selling book, *The Mystery of Capital*, was described by *The Economist* as 'the most intelligent book yet written about the current challenge of establishing capitalism in the developing world'.[5] De Soto's case is that 'despite capitalism's triumph over communism, the market system is in deep trouble as long as so much of the world remains excluded.[6] The key to both spurring development and securing capitalism is enabling tens of millions of [excluded] entrepreneurs across the third world to become part of the system rather than excluded from it by bureaucracy and red tape.'[7]

His work comes with solutions, too. A critical first step towards inclusion is the establishment of clear, enforceable property rights. Such reforms enable individuals to formalise their assets and leverage them to obtain credit – an essential ingredient for entrepreneurship and upward mobility. In a nutshell, De Soto argues property rights plus limited but smart regulation, plus efficient, profit-motivated banks, build prosperity.

Here, a side note is important. The shift from describing individuals or communities as 'poor' to referring to them as 'excluded' is not merely a semantic change; it is a deliberate move to uphold and respect human dignity. This language permeates Tyme's beliefs and behaviour. The term 'poor' often carries a connotation of deficiency or inferiority, inadvertently defining people by their economic status alone. It risks reducing complex human experiences and potential to a single dimension of need or lack.

In contrast, the term 'excluded' reframes the narrative. It acknowledges that the circumstances of poverty are often the result of systemic barriers – whether they be economic, social or political – which prevent individuals from accessing opportunities, resources and platforms for participation. By focusing on exclusion, we shift the perspective from personal deficit to systemic weaknesses or failings, highlighting that a key element of achieving inclusion and equity is about fixing systems and institutions, rather than about addressing people's capabilities.

This approach is rooted in the notion of dignity. Every person, regardless of their socioeconomic status, possesses inherent worth and deserves to be a full participant in society. When we speak of 'exclusion', we emphasise the importance of creating pathways for people to engage fully in economic, social and cultural life. It is a call to action to remove barriers and create environments where everyone can thrive.

Ultimately, language shapes perception. By choosing 'excluded' over 'poor', we help reinforce the idea that dignity is not conditional upon wealth or status but is a fundamental human right. It also aligns with a more hopeful and proactive stance, focusing on inclusion and opportunity rather than deficit and dependence. And this is the language of Tyme.

Returning to the point, together Prahalad and De Soto provide a foundation for the design of banking models that benefit us all. It involves rethinking the entire value chain of financial inclusion – from legal and regulatory reforms that protect property rights to business strategies that target the underserved. When banks successfully incorporate these elements, they can foster a virtuous cycle where increased access to finance spurs entrepreneurship, which, in turn, creates jobs and generates economic growth, which feeds the well-being of households and strengthens the social fabric. In this way, this cycle not only uplifts individuals, but it also contributes to broader societal progress.

Ultimately, the contributions of Prahalad and De Soto reinforce the idea that banking is not solely about profit margins – it is fundamentally about empowering people. Their models illustrate that when the financial system becomes truly inclusive, it can serve as a powerful engine for economic growth and social development. By bridging the gap between formal finance and the needs of the marginalised, banks can transform 'dead capital' into a dynamic force for progress, driving innovation and inclusivity in tandem.

Banks boost growth

It may seem trite to some that a good banking system fosters economic growth. More exactly, the better a banking system, the faster a national economy grows – with the infamous economic caveat, all else being equal. Ross Levine of Stanford University illustrates this with his seminal paper in the *Journal of Economic Literature*.[8] This vast review of empirical data and theoretical positions finds that the quality of the banking system is a strong predictor of rates of economic growth, capital accumulation and technological change.

To develop the argument further, there is a strong, positive relationship between a country's saving rate measured as a percentage of gross domestic product (GDP) and countries' growth rates. In a study covering 60 years of data, the evidence shows that for 160 countries, the saving rate explains about half of economic growth. Countries with high saving rates have high growth rates, because saving funds investment, which fuels growth.[9] Here, there are two important asides.

The first aside is that there is a 'sweet spot' in terms of the saving and investment rate – and the evidence suggests that figure sits at around 30% of GDP for an emerging economy.[10] Rates that are much higher lead to underconsumption and overinvestment (China in recent years), and rates that are much lower translate into overconsumption and underinvestment (South Africa over the past 15 years).

The second aside is that there are only three sources of saving in the domestic economy: government, companies and households. A widely held belief is that in low-income economies, people are too 'poor' to save. This simply is nonsense. Every country that has a high income today was once a low-income economy and, even more importantly, it is household saving that plays a pivotal role in almost every 'economic miracle'.

Establishing savings pools is often constrained by missing institutions – reliable banks, enforceable property rights and stable legal frameworks are frequently absent or inaccessible. In their place, predatory financial actors thrive. These include loan sharks, locally known in parts of South Africa as *mashonisas*, who operate informally with opaque terms and exploitative practices. Such lenders typically charge exorbitant interest rates, often exceeding 200% annually, and enforce repayment through coercion, public shaming or threats of violence.

It is within this context that TymeBank's GrantAdvance takes on deeper significance. More than 25 million South Africans rely on some form of government income support, and while social grants are meant to protect the most vulnerable, they rarely come with access to responsible financial tools. This gap is what keeps *mashonisas* in business. As Cheslyn Jacobs, TymeBank's chief commercial officer, notes, 'The problem of debt among social grant recipients is a real one,' and without viable alternatives, 'many are forced into exploitative loan agreements with high interest charges.' GrantAdvance was designed to interrupt this cycle – providing early access to social grants without any fees or interest, precisely to reduce reliance on informal credit. It is a structural countermeasure, not just a product: one that acknowledges the fragile financial positions many South Africans face, while actively offering a safer, dignified alternative.

Pontsho Ramontsha, communications manager at TymeBank, explains how GrantAdvance allows grant beneficiaries who receive their social grants into a TymeBank EveryDay account to access an interest-free advance in the days leading up to their grant payment. GrantAdvance is typically available during the last ten days of the month and comes with no additional fees or interest, provided the amount is repaid when the next grant payment is received from the South African Social Security Agency (SASSA). Whatever was advanced is automatically deducted from the customer's EveryDay account once the grant lands. The service is available to general grant recipients (excluding Social Relief of Distress recipients) who have received at least one prior grant payment into their TymeBank account. It is widely used by those supporting dependants – 12% are pensioners and 7% are disability grants.

Usage patterns point to a combination of demand and urgency: about 30% of transactions take place on the morning GrantAdvance opens, and 60% to 70% occur on the first day of the cycle. This sharp uptake underscores the acute cash flow needs among South Africa's most vulnerable households – and the vital role that timely, low-friction banking solutions can play. 'This is not banking as usual,' says Ramontsha. 'This is banking built for inclusion – and for impact at scale.'

This makes inclusive banking systems a vital element in establishing household savings that fund investment, fuel economic growth and feed the social fabric. The risks of keeping cash under the proverbial mattress are so high that spending the money is often more attractive. With this evidence behind us, it is tragic that many people in developing nations don't even live close enough to a bank to have the simplest of savings accounts. Half of the adult population of Colombia, Indonesia, Argentina, Kenya and Peru don't have bank accounts. Two-thirds of the adult population of Nigeria, Mexico, the Philippines, Egypt, Vietnam and Morocco don't have bank accounts.[11] In South Sudan, the figure stands at 91%.[12] These figures, read against an understanding of the impact of financial inclusion, is what fashions the mission of Jonker and Van der Walt, and the purpose of Tyme.

Microfinance, macro impact

Even today, one of the most striking examples of banks fostering financial inclusion is the microfinance revolution pioneered by Muhammad Yunus and the Grameen Bank in Bangladesh (now with operations around the world).[13] Grameen, launched in the wake of Bangladesh's 1974 famine, provides microloans almost exclusively to impoverished individuals in rural areas. Grameen replaced informal moneylenders that frequently charted interest rates of up to 200% per annum. It provided formal bank loans carrying an interest charge of 20%.

Well over 90% of Grameen's clients are women and the average loan is just US$100. Most importantly, the bank lends without the need for any physical or financial collateral. It turns out, a social contract is a sufficiently powerful force. Recoveries are over 95%. The bank captures the scope for their model to create impact as follows: 'One billion women around the world are excluded from the financial system. If women were able to start and scale new businesses at the same rate men do, economic gains would be over US$5 trillion a year.'[14]

Empirical research on microcredit in Bangladesh shows that access to finance leads to measurable improvements in living standards and a reduction in income inequality.[15] This evidence underscores the transformative power of banks when they target underserved markets and tailor financial products to local needs. Finance is contextual, and clearly the Grameen Bank is a case that guides Tyme.[16]

Banking on technology: The 'and' of digital banking

If banks matter, digital banks are the great enabler. The digitisation of banking services has transformed how people interact with their finances, making access faster, easier and more inclusive. But this same transformation has also introduced new vulnerabilities.

'We have become the target of scammers because of our size,' says Albert (Abet) Tinio, co-CEO of GoTyme Bank. 'In the last two weeks of December 2024, there were 494 clients who were scammed using what we've come to call "mall backpack towers".' The scam was as simple as it was effective. Fraudsters walked through shopping malls with modified backpacks containing portable signal-boosting devices – essentially miniature cell towers disguised in everyday bags. These rogue towers hijacked nearby mobile connections, allowing scammers to intercept SMS-based one-time passwords (OTPs) and gain access to mobile banking sessions. It was a textbook case of social engineering meeting technological subversion – and a reminder that scale brings not just reach, but risk. Tinio is clear about the bank's response: '494 is a very small number, but it's 494 too many.'

The challenges and opportunities posed by digital transformation are central to current debates on the future of money and banking.

Digital financial inclusion (DFI) sparks a virtuous cycle. Data from the Association of Southeast Asian Nations (ASEAN) confirms this. 'DFI accelerates the ASEAN banking stability which not only decreases the default risk of the banks but also upturns the financial mobility in the region. The results also suggest that ASEAN banks are, with the implementation of DFI, likely to uphold the banking sector stability by reducing liquidity crisis and non-performing loans.'[17]

An impact report by BlueEarth Capital illustrates the significance of TymeBank's role in expanding access to digital financial services in South Africa.[18] According to the report, 13% of customers were entirely new to banking, while 67% had no viable banking alternatives before joining

TymeBank. The report also highlights that 42% of TymeBank's customers reside in rural areas, a share significantly higher than the national rural population average of around 30%, confirming the bank's success in reaching underserved communities. Customers cited meaningful improvements in their financial lives: 80% reported lower banking costs, and 73% experienced a better quality of life due to more convenient, accessible services. At the time of the report, TymeBank had also onboarded approximately 75,000 small and micro-enterprises, 74% of which identified the bank's flexible, unsecured working capital as a key factor in improving their growth and profitability.

However, the benefits of digital banking are not being shared equally. While emerging nations in Asia have been particularly good at adopting and improving digital financial services to slash poverty, the results indicate that 'in developing countries, a persistent divide exists between gender, the wealthy and the poor, and urban and rural areas regarding access to and usage of digital financial services'.[19] There is much work to be done. In Jonker's words, 'We are scratching at the surface of the human potential still to be unleashed.'

Part III

The First Tyme

Chapter 5

When Two Worlds Collide

Life can only be understood backwards; but it must be lived forwards.
— Søren Kierkegaard

Louis Geeringh counted two of South Africa's biggest companies – Standard Bank and MTN – among his clients. When it became clear that Coen Jonker's vision couldn't be realised within Standard Bank's structures, Geeringh invited the lawyer-turned-guerrilla-banker to join him as a partner at Deloitte Consulting in September 2011. 'It cost me a lot of money to buy Coenraad out of Standard Bank, which still hurts me to this day,' he quips.

Jonker's move aligned neatly with the sale of his friend Tjaart van der Walt's data analytics business, C-Sense, to General Electric. Jonker, who had invested in C-Sense as part of a 'friends-and-family' round in 2001, also received a payout. The pair had built on their university acquaintance over the years, co-invested in several ventures, played pivotal roles at each other's weddings and had developed a profound respect for each other's skills – underpinned by an unhesitating trust in each other.

'When Coen shared his frustration over dinner one night about trying to build Community Banking within Standard Bank, I challenged him to go it alone and he asked whether I would partner with him. The answer was obvious. We agreed that we were going to build a multi-country bank for emerging markets even before he resigned from Standard Bank and started talking to Louis Geeringh. He had learnt banking, had a good understanding of the regulatory issues and was ready to do something new. We did it on a handshake and even had a photo taken to commemorate the moment. That is now lost, but we undertook to work together,' says Van der Walt, who would also join the team at Deloitte, insisting he not be paid until there was some revenue to be had. He set about researching the fast-growing and emerging digital banking environment, quickly realising that its success would depend entirely on the quality of information the new venture would be able to harvest from its clients. That was precisely what he was good at.

In the meantime, Jonker barely had time to settle into his new life as a consultant before being whisked off to meet the MD of MTN South Africa, Karel Pienaar. Geeringh informally floated the idea of a banking collaboration between Deloitte and MTN in the car park following the meeting. Pienaar expressed interest and that was enough to set the wheels in motion. After all, Vodafone had revolutionised financial services in Kenya with the launch of M-Pesa in 2007, leapfrogging moribund legacy banks and allowing microfinance to meaningfully impact the lives of its customers. It transformed Kenya's economy, driving financial inclusion from 26% in 2006 to over 80% today. Not only did it have a direct positive impact on citizens, but it demonstrated the power of African innovation and the ability of home-grown solutions to bridge infrastructure gaps and empower entire populations.

The subtext was that MTN was missing a trick and Geeringh had a solution. Teaming up made sense. On paper at least. Nothing, however, is as clear-cut as it seems.

For Pienaar, the opportunity of adding banking services to MTN's existing mobile offering was a no-brainer. Pienaar was described in 2011 by technology news website TechCentral as a 'wanderer and workaholic', who had been instrumental in the group's rapid expansion into new markets. The publication described him as 'a smiling but imposing figure whose name commands respect in the halls of the company's gleaming 14th Avenue head office in Fairlands, Johannesburg'.

If anyone was going to get the idea, it was him. Pienaar had been with the firm since before it was granted its licence to operate, and he knew it inside out. This was not MTN's first rodeo. It had tried and failed to do versions of financial services previously, including in its flailing MTN Banking venture with Standard Bank. Pienaar was open to new ideas to drive more traffic over an expensive-to-maintain mobile network that was already beginning to show signs of slowing, as average revenue per user was under pressure and the firm would need alternative sources of revenue into the future.

The pitch to MTN was to build a regulated standalone money transfer service called Mobile Money – and they committed to do it within six months. Jonker's powers of persuasion are legendary, and he is at his best when pitching an idea to potential investors. It was a bold offer and a gargantuan task. MTN committed R60 million to the venture via a project fee, and Geeringh diverted the efforts of his entire core banking team in return for a 25% equity stake in the bank. Pienaar took the idea to group CEO Sifiso Dabengwa, who gave it the green light and 'Project Ubiquity' was born.

'MTN is a completely federated organisation, meaning nothing you do in South Africa is necessarily true for what they do in Uganda, Nigeria or Ghana, where executives in those counties make their own decisions, which makes it very difficult to roll out a single solution across multiple geographies,' says Geeringh. Not that they were focused on the multi-country opportunity the tie-up might bring at this point – they were simply intent on getting started.

Jonker worked on the substance of what a cellphone bank might look like, with the benefit of building from scratch using the knowledge gleaned not just from books and the models of other successful operators but also the hard lessons learnt at Standard Bank.

'Race Day', or launch, was set for 26 June 2012, and the plan was to descend on downtown Johannesburg at rush hour, open accounts and issue cards using Android tablets to connect to the Home Affairs database and load money onto them in real time, perform card transactions through any card-acquiring device and withdraw cash from any ATM. It was an evolution of the approach developed at Community Banking and was designed to avoid the friction in the MTN Banking model that had hindered its growth.

First, they needed a bank licence. Applying for a new licence was costly, cumbersome and time-consuming. Besides, the South African Reserve Bank had not issued one since Capitec a decade before. With the 2008 global financial crisis and its own small banks' implosion still fresh in its institutional memory, being the first applicant in ten years was more trouble than it was worth, especially when you could simply rent one from a bank that had already done the hard yards with the regulator.

The terms offered by the South African Bank of Athens appeared the most reasonable. Geeringh ensured that the licence agreement was signed between MTN and the Bank of Athens to avoid any suggestion of a conflict of interest.

They assembled what Geeringh refers to as a 'coalition of the willing' and the team moved to what Dominique Collett, who by now had also left Standard Bank to join the venture, describes as a 'funny little office' within the multi-acre Deloitte campus, but far enough away to work without undue interference. 'It was a dump,' says John Kane, 'but it had a great vibe; we had a graffiti artist come in and do murals of our ambitions all over the walls.'

Van der Walt had the practical experience of building businesses from the ground up and set about building an entity with a solid framework. This is where the dinner-table lessons with his father kicked in: 'He taught me that a good business can fail on a poor administrative backbone.' He hired the best administrator he knew. Issie de Bruyn had ensured nothing was out of place at C-Sense and set about doing the same for the new venture. In addition to Collett, others joined from Standard Bank, including Kane, who had run operations at Community Banking, and Cheslyn Jacobs, who had joined the outfit while on a rotation through Standard Bank as a young graduate trainee. The Deloitte team included Tauriq Keraan, who had consulted to Standard Bank, and a visionary technologist called Ockert Harms, who had a decade-long track record of building core banking systems.

'Ockert is by far the best chief technology officer I have ever worked with,' says Collett, who now runs her own venture capital firm investing in fintechs across Africa. 'He had the unusual combination of deep technical knowledge, the ability to build commercial offerings and he puts teams together like nobody else I know.'

With a rented licence secured, the team set about building an early iteration of the bank. The Standard Bank experience had taught them that distribution and marketing would be vital to converting cellphone customers to bank customers, and work started with MTN's head of marketing, Serame Taukobong – today CEO at Telkom Limited, the listed telecommunications group.

Things were proceeding as planned but didn't last long.

The fact that Deloitte held a 25% stake in the new venture wasn't a problem until it was flagged as a potential conflict of interest by the head office in New York, which had secured the contract to audit the National Bank of Greece, the 100% shareholders of the South African Bank of Athens. The global financial crisis had heightened awareness around conflicts of interest, real or perceived, and when the bosses in New York heard about Geeringh's fledgling startup, all hell broke loose.

'This became a signature project for us. In time, the powers that be got to hear about it and, before I knew it, the Boeings started arriving with what I like to refer to as the "golden cufflinks" to tell me that I had to give up the equity stake,' says Geeringh. The memory still rankles more than a decade later. 'There were countless discussions. I aged ten years, lost most of the middle section of my hair and the argument. I was forced to take a letter to MTN rescinding our right to the free equity stake because of independence.'

On top of that, the project team was to be evicted from Deloitte property and Geeringh was instructed to have those on the team removed from the payroll in two weeks. Geeringh and Jonker convinced MTN to shift the contract from Deloitte to a new entity, but the big company baulked at the idea of taking on staff, plus there was a new nervousness about taking the risk of a bank onto the mobile operator's balance sheet.

Taukobong recalls first presenting the problem to Pienaar before escalating it to the MTN Group CEO, Sifiso Dabengwa, who also baulked at rushing new hires: 'Are you running a bloody spaza shop? You can't just hire people on a whim,' challenged Dabengwa, when presented with the problem that the team that was building its platform might have to shut down without support. Deloitte paid salaries to the end of June; they were then on their own, despite continuing to rent premises on the firms' campus until they moved to MTN.

It was a serious blow and left the founders with a painful choice – give up before they really started or fund it themselves.

'Coen, Louis and I met at Irene Country Lodge, where we discussed our options. Louis committed in a very high integrity way to underwrite the Deloitte team members for three months and said they would still have their old jobs if they wanted to go back. But Coen and I had to fork out the capital to launch the new venture,' recalls Van der Walt. 'We did it by selling the consulting project to MTN, which only paid the bulk of our invoices five months later, and by getting friends and family to invest. We managed to raise about R15 million.'

It didn't yet have a name – that would come later in the year on the suggestion of team member, American-born Michelle Gervais, who later went on to become global head of Data Policy and Governance at Visa. TYME, short for Take Your Money Everywhere, had been used by a pioneer in shared electronic funds transfer (EFT) systems in the US state of Wisconsin in 1975 and had fallen out of use. It came with a price tag. They pondered for a while and in early 2013 paid US$25,000 for Tyme.com. This was the official start of what would become Tyme, but not before Van der Walt contributed about 60% of the spoils of the money he earned from the sale of C-Sense, while Jonker found money to make up his contribution by liquidating properties and other assets, as well as the full sale proceeds of his share in Van der Walt's business.

The pair were taking a gamble and told the small team they planned to take with them that they could promise no more than two months' salary to the 17 individuals selected for the next stage of the development of the business. Despite that, not one of them declined the invitation.

An 18th person demanded to join the small group and appealed to Van der Walt to hire him, but he was turned down on the basis that the firm had no money to stump up for another wage.

'I always back myself as having a great eye for top talent. In this instance, my absolute obsession to ensure we pulled through financially pushed me in the wrong direction,' concedes Van der Walt.

But Nate Clarke was not about to be easily fobbed off. He had been working as a management consultant for Deloitte in 2010 when he attended a mobile money conference in Washington, DC and first learnt about M-Pesa: 'I knew when I met the founders that this technology was going to change the world.' In February 2012, en route to investigate a mobile health project in Tanzania, he caught wind of a 'top-secret' mobile money project taking shape in South Africa. It was radical by Deloitte standards, and he convinced the partner to whom he reported in the US to allow him to travel to South Africa as an observer on the project. He was captivated by what the founders wanted to build and informed them he would be joining the team. 'I really didn't care at that point whether they paid me or not; I needed to be part of it.' He took Jonker on a walk through the parkland grounds of the Deloitte campus and convinced him to make room for him. To show his commitment, he left his bags at the office and returned briefly to the US to tidy up his affairs.

'Coen and Nate convinced me that he should be hired. We could not have made a better decision,' says Van der Walt.

In addition to Clarke and Van der Walt, there were five people on the team who had worked together at Standard Bank: Coen Jonker, Cheslyn Jacobs, Tauriq Keeran, John Kane and Dominique Collett. The remaining nine were the critical technology team required to build the bank, led by Ockert Harms, who brought them across from Deloitte. Jonker and Van der Walt made 30% of the equity in the business available to this startup team and reserved a further 10% as an incentive scheme.

Since MTN opted not to commit to the project, the mobile operator ceded over to Tyme the intellectual property associated with the operating model and technology developed up to that point.

PART III: THE FIRST TYME

The earliest data centres were on-premise – the cloud would come later.

They leased an off-the-shelf banking platform from Direct Transact, a business established in 2002 to provide Banking-as-a-Service and Payments-as-a-Service technology to aspirant bankers. Over time, it would service three-quarters of the country's clearing and settlement banks. Van der Walt agreed to its terms of conditions, despite a demanding price point. 'There was no choice, they were the only game in town, but they didn't understand our lower-cost model. We used the platform at the start as we prepared for Race Day. In the two weeks prior to launch, we had to close out contracts with all our suppliers, including Direct Transact, and I warned them then that we would leave as soon as we could.'

The model they developed required banking technology, access to customers, which came from MTN, and a retail partner to provide a place where customers could sign up, be issued a card and have access to till points to access cash.

There were three primary contenders that might act as retail partners.

Van der Walt knew key players at Pepkor, which years before had tried a kiosk model with some of the founders of Capitec in an early iteration, but that didn't come to fruition. 'We also went a long way down the path with Shoprite, but they went with Absa instead,' remembers Collett. It was in food retailer Pick n Pay that they found alignment with an executive named Matt Bresler, who was eager to replace the group's existing money transfer system and agreed to adopt the MTN Mobile Money offering.

It was a critical breakthrough.

MTN was still paying a project fee, albeit smaller than the amount agreed with Deloitte, R17 million for three projects, and the team was doing additional consulting for the company to make ends meet. The team warned it would not go live unless it had a retail partner. The founders also brought Rolf Eichweber on board and named him as a co-founder. His expertise was grounded in eight years at Standard Bank. While he had not been involved in Community Banking, he had experience in distribution, operations and customer strategy, and he had risen to director for Financial Inclusion and Electronic Channels for Africa. He would later briefly run the bank during a tumultuous period in its evolution, after which he would leave to do his own thing.

While Jonker busied himself in keeping relations with MTN functioning and overseeing the building of the bank, Van der Walt created the structure of the enterprise, ensuring that if it did fail, it would not be because its back office and administration had been inadequate. Another key aspect of the creation of Tyme, Van der Walt recalls, was the design principles that would shape its thinking around how to build the technology that would not only drive the MTN venture but would also shape future iterations of its offering.

'This was one of those areas where Coen and my partnership really came to the fore. Many of the design principles had already been established during the Standard Bank years. But I had the lean startup experience with an entrepreneurial gene, while Coen had the institutional know-how and the accompanying boardroom savvy. We knew that we could plan and design a bank that would break the shackles of a big institution at a cost that was unheard of,' says Van der Walt.

The core principles ensured that no Tyme employee would handle cash – that would be done by retail staff at till points. Cash was cumbersome and costly to handle, but the founding team knew it was central to serving its customers, so it focused on providing the most 'ubiquitous' cash access model available in the market at the time. Retailers were happy to collaborate. Any cash they were able to issue to customers reduced the volume of notes and coins that needed to be shifted on a daily basis, which had the benefit of lowering their cost. It also reduced the risk of that money being stolen in transit. When it came to lending, the business should operate with a central set of rules that were automated to give a speedy response to an applicant without the cost and friction of a credit committee approval for each transaction. That obsessive focus on cost containment meant that the business should not require a single sheet of paper to be used anywhere and it was not to have brick-and-mortar infrastructure of its own. And for Kane, any machine he built needed to be able to sign up a customer and issue a personalised card within five minutes.

PART III: THE FIRST TYME

There is a running joke within the senior management at Tyme that January is the most frightening time of the year as it comes after Jonker's annual holiday, during which he invariably reads books that challenge his thinking. In December 2011, he read up on industrial design and 3D printing and turned to Kane to deliver a speedy prototype of a machine that could be replicated and distributed quickly and efficiently. It would need customers to be able sign up with little or no assistance, which would be available in the form of a dedicated employee serving as an ambassador in a retail environment. Part of the ambassador's job was to interest a potential customer to sign up, answer questions about the bank and its products, and finally provide support to input their information if they needed it. If the machine could do the work, things would be considerably simpler, and if the customer could go through the process unassisted, they felt less intimidated to transact into the future.

The Standard Bank experience had taught the team what didn't work. Any system they developed would eventually have to be automated and able to independently verify the identity of the applicant, make a credible assessment of their creditworthiness, log a home address and issue a numbered debit card with their name on it – but that was some way off.

The MTN deal solved the first part of the problem – it gave them access to millions of potential customers, but that alone would not be enough to ensure a successful roll-out. Standard Bank's insistence that Community Banking be integrated into the group and use the branch network not only had a cost impact, but restricted where it could operate. Retailers, however, enjoyed a far wider physical footprint.

Internally, the team called it 'Project Ubiquity'. Kane blushes at the name now, but at the time the idea was that they were going to make financial services as ubiquitous as mobile communications. They even had a mock-up of a bank card branded 'Ubiquity'. Kane's biggest lesson from that time: 'Never use words that your customers and half your staff don't understand.'

However, it was scrappy at the start, and the first machines were basic. They used Unstructured Supplementary Service Data (USSD) technology and, with Reserve Bank approval, used a lower standard of customer verification. That restricted what the customer could do using the platform and also restricted the value and volume of money they could put through their accounts.

'This got us lots of customers but was inherently risky; we onboarded bad actors, but the limits prevented them from doing lots of damage,' says Kane. It wasn't perfect, but it was working. The first customers could not be issued cards but could use their phones to transfer money. It was groundbreaking, as money could be transferred between accounts and cash could be deposited and withdrawn at Pick n Pay tills. MTN telco services could also be purchased – this would later expand to other mobile operators.

They urgently needed to up limits and add cards, but that required a higher level of permission from the Reserve Bank. They needed an inexpensive way to standardise the customer identification process, which had to be done reliably by untrained staff, who also needed to link cards to customers' accounts in-store.

This eventually would lead to the creation of a device Kane proudly labelled the 'Tyme Machine'. Kane set about developing the first machines for use in Pick n Pay and Boxer stores – initially a clunky combination of publicly available technologies that would evolve over time to form the backbone of what he labelled its 'phygital' (a mix of physical and digital) strategy. It is hard to imagine today, less than a decade later, that touchscreen smartphones were still new to the market and the preserve of wealthier individuals, so the obvious path to customer onboarding, using an app and biometric verification, was not viable at the time.

Globally, digital-first banks had simply gone to market without any physical market presence. That might have worked in more sophisticated markets that had high levels of digital literacy, but South Africa in 2013, and even today, would need more than an ad popping up on Instagram to convince someone to open an account. The value of the kiosks would be demonstrated over the next decade, first in South Africa and later in the Philippines, where the kiosks remain the primary source of customer sign-up. However, as consumers have become increasingly confident to deal with more complex mechanisms like independently signing on via an application, that reliance is reducing.

The earliest machines were rudimentary – little more than android tablets with a cellphone mechanism enabling users of the early kiosk to connect to credit bureaus and the Department of Home Affairs via the mobile network. The machines had a camera function that allowed a picture of an identity document to be scanned and captured and the data shared with the government database. Later versions enabled fingerprints to be taken as a further means of verification and also provided customers with the opportunity to select their address based on information held by credit bureaus. Their true superpower, however, was that they were in places potential customers already trusted and visited routinely – supermarkets with till points served as the ideal technology for depositing and withdrawing cash. There was an added advantage that the stores were secure, so not only were the machines protected, but there was also a safe space from which ambassadors could operate.

Regulators who were eager to see more citizens in the digital economy saw the result as a win-win.

All prospective customers needed to be in possession of their green government-issued bar-coded ID book, which they placed on the machine, where a smartphone positioned at exactly the right distance from the document would ensure that it could be accurately captured without the risk of human error. The user would then be prompted to turn the device to face them, where it would snap an image of themselves. That information was submitted to a back office, so that a physical check could be made and their fingerprint connected to the application. Its first iterations were costly and a time-consuming process that later technologies would automate. The earliest versions, as groundbreaking as they were, were anything but seamless.

Another issue was that the people signing up the customers in the early days of the relationship with Pick n Pay were retail staff, not working for the bank. Because of issues from shift rosters to staff churn, the team found itself in an endless cycle of staff training on a service that had little visibility beyond it being delivered at the cigarette counter. It was fine if you knew it was there, but the staff had other demands, from delivering consumer nicotine fixes to selling lottery tickets. Opening a bank account was hardly front of mind for customer or staff member. Interestingly, the same issue hobbled PEP Bank more than a decade before. Store managers resented the fact that its machines trialled by Boland Bank, the leaders of which later built Capitec, used valuable floor space that could have been used to move clothing.

'We onboarded a lot of customers, but it drove us all mad. I am from a process engineering background from heavy industry, so this idea of multiple levels of non-replicability always irritated me enormously,' says Kane.

The group's original development lab still operates from a building tucked away in Johannesburg's Rosebank commercial district, where software and hardware design take place for the continuous development of the phygital model. The kiosks that are now used in other parts of the world are designed by South Africans in the country, and the innovation team uses laser cutters, 3D printers and scanners to shape future machines.

This was groundbreaking stuff. The team studied models that had enjoyed some success elsewhere, including one offering in Brazil that used the owners of remote stores as agents of the bank. There was also the model used by supermarket giant Tesco in the UK, which had enjoyed success starting its own bank using till points as a mechanism to deposit and withdraw cash.

The team went live with MTN Mobile Money on 22 November 2012. The entire day and night of the 22nd and into the early morning of the 23rd was spent negotiating the final terms of the deal between Tyme and MTN, with the then chief marketing officer of South Africa, Brian Gouldie. He went on to become a strong supporter of Tyme and later became the CEO of MTN in Uganda. It was made even more memorable because it was Jonker's birthday and Kane's wedding anniversary and, most famously, it was also the day that a former Deloitte staffer called Anthony Bezos was heard exclaiming loudly: 'I can't believe the fucking thing works!'

'We had 10,000 customers in the first week of MTN Mobile Money,' says Kane.

There was already some strategic disagreement, however. While the team kept improving the technology and the platform, they were not able to convince MTN to a fuller proposition. They saw M-Pesa in Kenya as an ideal model, but Tyme wanted to build banking services and not simply deliver digital wallets for shifting cash, as they were increasingly commonplace and did not give them a competitive edge.

They needed a full banking licence to prove they could do it and also execute on their vision to build a multi-country banking group. Things were moving too slowly for their liking in South Africa, but Van der Walt had family connections in Namibia, and they knew of an opportunity to apply for a licence there with people who knew the market. He met with his brother Daneel and his Pointbreak partners in July 2012, just after the formal birth of what would later be called Tyme. There was a meeting of minds, design commenced soon thereafter, and a partnership agreement was finalised between Tyme and Pointbreak a few months later. In November 2014, two years later, EBank was launched to the public with its own bank licence. The partnership between Pointbreak and Tyme was again built on the foundations of purpose and utmost trust.

EBank with bright pink standout branding (not to be confused with the moniker that was no longer in use at Standard Bank) was first switched on in August 2013 and operated under a provisional banking licence before receiving its full licence nine months later. Regulators could see the benefit of having a branchless digital bank in the sparsely populated country of Namibia.

'This was where we really refined the Tyme Machine concept and delivered a device that could be run by our own agent in the field,' says Kane. Namibia's EBank demonstrated to the team they could go it alone.

The Standard Bank lessons of going to where there were no branches and teaming up with smaller local retailers paid off. They went to places that were simply not viable for traditional banks to go at that point. Within six months, about 10% of the bankable population in the country had signed up.

It was this model that first brought Tyme to the attention of the Commonwealth Bank of Australia, which was expanding beyond its own borders, growing rapidly in Southeast Asia and looking at several options in South Africa for expansion … and happened upon Tyme.

Chapter 6

A Pure Digital Plan

Try again. Fail again. Fail better.
— Samuel Beckett

Commonwealth Bank of Australia (CBA) was not only that country's most valuable financial institution but also its biggest company and its biggest employer; it ranked among the top 20 banks globally by market capitalisation.

It dominated retail banking and wealth management and was a domestic force in what it billed as 'institutional services', covering corporate lending, trading and complex financial solutions. Australia had emerged from the global financial crisis in good shape, and CBA stood as a symbol of resilience – although not all was as it seemed. When it first approached Tyme in 2014, CBA appeared at the height of its powers, but the business was straddling several significant fault lines that would ultimately fracture and once again threaten the very existence of Tyme.

For now, however, only a small handful of insiders at the Australian bank might have been aware of the impending tsunami. As far as Tyme could tell, CBA was massively profitable, had a robust balance sheet, was aggressively expanding into digital services and needed a platform to build off. In turn, Tyme needed a banking licence and a much deeper pool of capital from which to grow – partnering with the likes of CBA would help address those constraints.

So, despite some apprehension among its senior leadership who remembered the agony of its previous dalliances with institutional bureaucracy, the deal was agreed. The deal, valued at A$40 million (R365 million), meant a solid payday for senior members of the management team, most of whom agreed to a three-year earnout, with a further incentive via an equity derivative structure based on the team's outperformance relative to the CBA cost of capital.

Australia had long been a popular destination for South African emigrants who had built up a reputation for a strong work ethic in that country, but many of its companies, including Tyme's retail partner in South Africa, Pick n Pay, had been less successful in trying to establish themselves there. While it was quite normal to see investment flow from west to east as firms sought to diversify Down Under, it was highly unusual to see any Australian corporate interest in South African assets beyond the mining sector.

CBA had been scouring the globe for a digital banking model it could apply in Southeast Asia, where it was eager to grow its presence. Its researchers happened across EBank in Namibia and liked what they saw. EBank was ideally suited to the environment, as it offered Namibians their first chance to bank via their cellphones. Regulators had approved the licence quickly, eager to introduce affordable alternatives into the market, and the team established trusted relationships with local retailers, giving the bank a physical presence. Its dazzling neon-pink colour scheme was eye-catching and, like the proposition, not something that had been seen in banking before.

However, CBA had no interest in owning a bank in a country dominated by a vast desert landscape and population thinly spread across an expansive geography. (The irony was not lost on the Tyme team, either.) So, a key condition of the deal was that Tyme had to sell it's 38.3% stake in Namibia's EBank. The stake reverted to Namibian investment company Pointbreak, part-owned by Tjaart van der Walt's brother, and two years later was sold to FNB Namibia, which used it to roll out its e-wallet in that country.

While the forced sale of EBank was painful, it did show that the Tyme team was onto something. They had a proof of concept that worked. By

2015, they had signed up 70,000 customers and secured a presence for their kiosks in 120 different retail outlets. Ockert Harms and his team had built a low-cost platform and core banking system with a total project cost of just R30 million from scratch and operated using on-premise servers to host its data. Former Deloitte consultant Theuns Botha had led the project to apply for the bank licence.

It was the country's seventh commercial bank, but CBA had bigger fish to fry. The scale of the Namibia opportunity was insufficiently attractive. It had bought Tyme for one thing only: the team and the knowledge it had of building a proven digital banking platform.

CEO Ian Narev announced the deal during its results presentation in February 2015: 'Tyme gives us new opportunities in our emerging markets footprint, as well as providing capability to enhance innovation in our core markets,' adding that it would be useful in helping it target emerging middle-class customers in countries like India, China and Vietnam. CBA was already a fintech leader and its app was highly regarded – it had 3 million customers who logged in 15 million times a week and carried out A$2.5 billion in transactions every seven days.

Its A$40-million investment was a small bet on a potentially large return.

Considering the many frustrations the Community Banking team had at Standard Bank, only to have Deloitte pull the plug on its MTN deal and the company later losing its enthusiasm for providing banking services to its cellphone customers, it may seem surprising that Jonker and Van der Walt even considered a deal with a larger and even more bureaucratic institution. However, the timing of the unsolicited approach proved to be fortuitous. By November that year, the MTN relationship was over. A new management team at MTN decided that even though Mobile Money had 5 million customers, it did nothing to advance its telco ambitions.

Van der Walt's scepticism about doing a deal with a large non-South African company was offset by the fact that the team as it was would not convince the Reserve Bank to issue them a licence without a large shareholder of record. The footprint of CBA in Southeast Asia could also be leveraged to fulfil the multi-country bank vision much sooner. Besides, they required capital to achieve their goals. And while he was not a corporate animal, Van der Walt took comfort from the fact that Jonker was adept at navigating institutional politics and understood better than most how big banks worked.

CBA insisted one of the senior Tyme directors be based in Hong Kong, home to its Southeast Asia hub. Jonker volunteered. It took a single phone call to his wife Kerry Anderson, who, despite not ever visiting the country, immediately agreed to relocate with their young daughters.

Van der Walt meantime busied himself using the EBank experience, as well as the cumulative institutional memory built from the numerous frustrations they had, first at Standard Bank and then at MTN, to establish some fundamental operating principles to govern the group's future expansion. They had proven the need for some kind of physical presence for a digital-first bank in a developing economy, and the retail partnership model where kiosks could be housed was key. They were also committed to the fact that no paper would be required throughout the customer experience and, if regulators demanded it, they would not enter those markets. Everything from signing up customers to all agreements had to be digital.

It took a while, but eventually the teams got the hang of it and the firm set about transforming its data into processed information and ultimately tools to help make it a quick and reliable processor of complex information.

Jonker stepped into a role that removed him from the day-to-day activities of Tyme. To some it might have appeared odd that Jonker was loosening his grip on the reins of the business he had dreamed up and talked into existence through multiple iterations, and now, just as its potential might be realised with the backing of one of the biggest banks in the world, he was leaving it to be managed by others, while he went to explore a brand-new opportunity. For Jonker, it was a strategic decision. He calculated he would be of greater use to the South African business if he wielded more influence within CBA. Besides, he would remain as chairperson of Tyme, and Van der Walt was still there, as was most of the core team who had been with him since the Standard Bank days and still held influential positions in the business.

Jonker was in his element, despite the demands of his schedule, which meant he was seldom home. He started as executive for digital banking, and by 2017 he was on the group's executive committee as head of CBA's International Financial Services Division, responsible for all its banking and insurance businesses outside of Australia and New Zealand, including China, Vietnam, Indonesia and India. He reported directly to group CEO Ian Narev, who openly sang the praises of his newest executive. The job was vast, complex and exciting, and Jonker seized the new opportunity with both hands. 'Of all the people I know, he is able to adapt to different places and cultures best,' says Van der Walt. Kerry recalls his being welcomed off a Cathay Pacific flight on one of his trips by the airline's head of public affairs, who greeted him with: 'I just wanted to meet the man who is doing more miles than any of our pilots.'

It soon became clear that China was not going to be an option for CBA, as its neobanks were developing fast and there were better opportunities elsewhere in the region. Jonker was quoted at the time as saying that the group would learn from that market but not compete in it. Australian media speculated at the time that Tyme might make Hong Kong its next market, after all it was the CBA hub, it was Jonker's home base and digital banking licences were in the offing.

Jonker had other ideas. His thinking reflected the principles drawn up by him and Van der Walt. While some regulators might have considered form-filling as little more than a trivial administrative requirement, Jonker regarded any unnecessary friction that slowed down the pace of customer acquisition, or made it more expensive, as a deal-breaker.

'It's a light footprint,' Jonker said at the time. 'Our ambition is to be purely digital, so the kiosks [which had been developed and were still being built in South Africa] are a stepping stone.' Jonker was learning everything he could about new markets, customers and the sorts of technology that was needed to make CBA's digital offerings appealing to them.

He quickly understood the imperative to offer full-service, day-to-day banking, matching existing banks but delivered seamlessly and quickly and at a much more compelling price point. There were already countless fintech players in the market that enabled money to be shifted across borders – competing there would be much harder. Core to the success of digital banks would be their ability to offer credit cards and other lending. It may be hard to comprehend now, but in 2017 fintechs and other so called 'digital banks' were not doing that.

There is also no quick fix to starting a bank in a new country. Other than the fact that it is hard to convince customers of your proposition, banks are tightly regulated entities in every country. Different regulators in different jurisdictions had vastly different requirements to ensure compliance. One small example that would prove pivotal to whether markets were to be considered was a requirement in some for so-called wet signatures, meaning customers needed to visit a branch to sign paper, while others required face-to-face meetings with prospective clients as a means for them to identify themselves effectively and ensure customers could be brought on board. It was going to be impossible to run a digital business in countries that were not digitised – one of the biggest constraints was that many did not have centralised digital ID databases, which enabled seamless onboarding of customers.

'Legacy tech systems are poisonous to the pure digital plan,' Jonker told *DigFin* in 2018.[1] Those legacy systems, however, solved the problems of cash deposits and withdrawals that the new players, like Tyme, still had to resolve.

Back in South Africa, the team set about making South Africa's first banking licence application in more than a decade and a half – a process that would take two years. During that time, they solidified the Pick n Pay partnership – first by signing a money transfer deal for a remittance product in May 2016 and later a ten-year distribution agreement in February 2017.

While CBA insisted on the sale of EBank as part of the deal, Jonker and Van der Walt stood firm on the fact that the first prototype to deliver on the new controlling shareholder's Southeast Asia ambitions should be built in South Africa. That decision would prove to be prescient. Prescient perhaps, but far from easy.

Chapter 7

Holding on for Dear Life

New beginnings are often disguised as painful endings.
— Lao Tzu

CBA sent a team of about 60 experienced Australian bankers to South Africa and, as was its prerogative, injected its own people into senior positions – it owned the business after all. Two worlds immediately collided.

'The Australians are not like the Brits,' says a former staff member. 'The Brits have been colonising people for centuries, so they have a unique way of being condescending towards you. But the Australians were just like straight-up awkwardly condescending.'

As much as there was a significant cultural misalignment between the teams right from the start, CBA did solve two fundamental problems for Tyme. The Australians brought with them the heft to add to a banking licence application and about R2 billion in capital, which it injected into the business. It also brought not just 'big-company' energy, but 'Australian big-company' rules and regulations. Australian corporate culture is a curious beast, made up of equal parts laid-back bonhomie and the rigorous application of rules and regulations. The South Africans, used to an environment where a red traffic light late at night is seen as a suggestion rather than an instruction, were not used to the application of rules that were not directly linked to the building of a bank.

Those who made the transition to the new management structure were struck by just how different the cultures were.

Early on, CBA sent two ergonomic specialists from Australia to teach staff how to sit properly in office chairs. When that intervention was deemed inadequate, the chairs were replaced, and the training repeated. 'They replaced perfectly good R2,500 chairs with R10,000 chairs,' says one former staff member, arguing that sort of expenditure had no place in a startup environment. In another case, the bank issued an instruction that no desks should be placed in direct sunlight due to the risks of UV exposure. If they were, those at those workstations should apply a high-factor sunscreen. The South Africans deemed it an unnecessary waste of time and resources, but the Australians were dead serious.

There were more substantive interventions, especially to the day-to-day working of the enterprise. The CBA board, for example, did not want direct responsibility for the field marketing business, which employed hundreds of first-time job seekers identified by the non-profit Harambee Youth Employment Accelerator. They acted as in-store ambassadors to help customers operate the kiosks that verified their identities, signed them up as customers and, at the time, issued money transfer wallets. The problem was that team members used the most cost-effective transport option available to them to get to and from work – South Africa's notorious minibus taxi. The board was concerned about the reputational implications if one of them was to be hurt or injured in an accident in a vehicle described locally as 'coffins on wheels' because of their poor safety record. While the exact origin of this phrase is unclear, a 2003 report by the International Labour Organization noted that the term was 'often applied to kombis', highlighting the long-standing nature of the concerns.[1]

CBA deemed the issue sufficient to raise at board level, as health and safety standards in the two markets were poles apart. Since the South African practices did not align with the Australian domestic standards, the board ordered the sale of the field marketing business to its management team and the establishment of an arms-length agreement between Tyme and the business that was known as Edge. This transaction alone added VAT of

14% and a profit margin of about 10% to the cost of field marketing – none of which went to those doing the actual work.

There were rules to be followed and boxes to be ticked. Lots of boxes. This operational risk aversion was reflected in the business itself. Even though CBA would exit before it had time to operate a bank in South Africa, it employed a team of 14 compliance officers without having a single account holder. Today, the group employs five compliance officers across its global operations.

The result was a series of, as Jonker puts it now, 'safe, suboptimal decisions', which included using technologies and processes that were standard in Australia but not suited to a more robust South African environment. 'It's not that we did anything fundamentally wrong, it was just not right for what we needed to achieve,' says Jonker.

'We lost our way and many in the founding team were pushed aside,' says Tauriq Keraan, who joined Tyme in the early days of its dealings with MTN. His broad view echoes that of others who were there at the time. Universally, there was a sense among the old guard that the business lost direction under CBA control. 'CBA was leading the build across different time zones, different teams and different geographies and that muddled accountability,' says Keraan. What had been a fast-moving, dynamic, experimental startup became bureaucratic and slow to adapt in a world where fintechs were rapidly evolving and the incumbents investing heavily to defend their dominance against a wave of startup competitors worldwide.'

'In hindsight, we were wrong to believe that Tyme would escape the bureaucracy and risk aversion of CBA as its investor. We thought that if we built the business on a different continent, far away from the mothership, it would enjoy some level of insulation from the bureaucratic culture in Australia,' concedes Jonker. However, that was not the case.

In the background, the team was furiously fulfilling the lengthy and demanding requirements for a banking licence. Then registrar of banks at the South African Reserve Bank, Kuben Naidoo, was especially receptive to applications from potential digital entrants. Global banking regulations had been tightened significantly following the global financial crisis, and the Basel III global regulatory framework had added withering levels of cost to running banking businesses, making it hard for new competitors to participate in the industry. However, new technologies were evolving rapidly, and lower-cost models were springing up in different parts of the world.

'I was of the view that it was possible to have a more competitive banking sector without it being unstable,' says Naidoo. South Africa had lost 17 banking licences in the early 2000s' crisis, which led to the dominance of the Big Four: Standard, FirstRand, Nedbank and Absa, with Investec offering specialist high-end services, and Capitec, initially at least, banking mostly lower-income earners and subsequently growing into the biggest retail bank in the country.

Naidoo's primary concern was to ensure the safety and soundness of the South African financial system, which is regarded globally as one of the best regulated in the world. That stiff regulation and the cost of operating a bank, however, had discouraged new investment.

The regulator was eager to inject fresh competition into the sector and invited applications to embark on a rigorous process of gaining approval to take customer deposits. Bank charges were considerably higher in South Africa than comparable economies, and competition was seen as key to bring down pricing.

Even though the regulator was eager to welcome new players, there was still a difficult application process to get through in terms of the Banks Act. The first requirement, governed by Section 13 of the Act, allows an applicant to establish a bank, appoint a board and staff, as well as internal and external auditors, while also signing up to the national payments system, which allows money to flow through the economy. It then took up to 18 months before a Section 16 application could be approved to start the operations of a fully fledged bank, and then a Section 17 application led to the granting of a licence.

'When we got the first license application in, I went to a colleague of mine, Neil Marais, at the Reserve Bank and asked where the department was that dealt with licences. He told me it did not exist, as there had been no application approved since 1999, so in some ways we had to learn how to process a bank licence application,' says Naidoo.

CBA argued for an international domicile for the holding company, even though its first operating entity would be a South African regulated domestic bank. The country's tough exchange control regime made this an imperative, as it could restrict its international expansion. The regulator agreed that it could be controlled from Hong Kong.

The Reserve Bank had cut its teeth on the foreign ownership of domestic banks when it approved London-based Barclays' 56% controlling stake in Absa in 2005. There was some concern that the regulator would object to Tyme's plan to use foreign-based cloud services to host its data. Previous regulators did not need to consider this issue, as banks operated their own substantial data centres inside the borders of South Africa. Tyme's timing was fortuitous. The incumbents had already been lobbying the regulator to use cloud services. The difference for Tyme was that cloud hosting was a business imperative and being able to host customer data was critical to it eventually becoming a multi-country digital bank. If Naidoo was going to allow the new applicants to use more cost-effective data storage options, he would be required to allow legacy players to do the same.

'We permitted South African banks to move to the cloud between 2017 and 2018 because we wanted to lower the capital costs of starting a bank. It would lower entry costs, and it would help to create a more level playing field,' says Naidoo, who gave the go-ahead once he was confident that there was a framework that enabled the regulator to retrieve data on the South African banking system irrespective of where it was kept.

Despite the ongoing licence application, and the potential it brought, all was not well inside the business. There was mounting dissatisfaction at the slow progress being made in building the digital infrastructure of the bank. It went through a series of rapid leadership changes. With Jonker out of the picture operationally, running the day-to-day of CBA's digital ambitions in Southeast Asia, CBA had appointed Rolf Eichweber as chief executive in January 2015. Eichweber was the former Standard Bank executive brought on board by the original founders at the start of the project with MTN. That did not last long. He shifted to becoming head of partnerships and

CBA appointed one of its own to run the project, Rowan Munchenberg, who stayed for about 18 months before being sent to run an Australian subsidiary. The group desperately needed stability and looked for an 'experienced banker' to do it.

Into the breach stepped 20-year Nedbank business banking veteran Sandile Shabalala, who found himself cast into the dysfunctional maelstrom in October 2016. It was a tall order to expect him to slip comfortably into the chaos of a new build. In traditional banks, orders flowed down from senior executives to those expected to do the work, while what Tyme needed was to be built from the ground up. CBA was leading the build, but the 'muddled accountabilities' referred to by Keraan were causing significant tensions in the business. The two main groups used different metrics to measure success. Van der Walt, who was overseeing all the group's technology operations, recalls the team being berated for 'not growing fast enough and not appointing people quickly enough'. In one case, by the end of 2015, shy of one year under CBA control, a senior executive prophesised that the 500-person headcount of the bank-being-built 'should be at 2,000' by the end of 2016.

Van der Walt was not wired that way. His way was about being lean and efficient, so, in early 2017, he left the business, frustrated with the continued disagreements on strategy. The bank was not being run in terms of his understanding of the original sale agreement.

Ockert Harms and his core team of tech developers also walked out to join the highly entrepreneurial FirstRand-owned direct insurance company, OUTsurance. Dominique Collett had joined FirstRand in mid-2014 soon after leaving Tyme, when the CBA deal was announced. Knowing Harms was increasingly frustrated with the CBA arrangement, Collett recommended 'the best chief technical officer I have ever worked with' as a logical choice for OUTsurance. The tech team departure was a severe blow, as it left a vacuum in tech development. But, as is so often the case in the Tyme story, it plays to the long-term advantage of the founders.

Harms was a brilliant operator, with a strong track record of building complex banking systems from scratch, but his refusal to brook interference from outside of his team and demanding they be housed separately from the rest of the office did lead to some disquiet among the less technically minded on the team. Van der Walt argues they would not have met the punishing deadlines put on them had they been more accessible.

'He delivered against the odds, at the speed of lightning and with superb quality. He had an incredible loyalty towards, and a sense of ownership of, Tyme. He trusted Coen and I unconditionally and knew we had his back. He had our backs as well. Plus, he had a great instinct about people and chose his team based on excellence and character. He just couldn't deal comfortably with mediocrity and kept everyone thinking on their feet.'

Collett and Van der Walt saw his genius, and it's a toss-up between them as to who is his number-one fan. 'I love Ockert, and we still meet up at least once a quarter,' says Van der Walt, whose own experience in developing digital technologies honed his appreciation of the skills Harms brought to the business. This was not only in writing code, but also in his ability to build strong, loyal teams that worked furiously – up to 140 hours a week – to deliver on demanding timelines. 'Once I was gone, I couldn't protect Ockert any more,' says Van der Walt.

Harms' strategy from the start was to guard his development team against what he regarded as unnecessary and fatuous interference. At Deloitte, he found a separate room at the office allocated to the project that was dubbed 'the black box' and denied access to anyone but the developers.

While Harms was talented at developing technologies to solve the problem of expensive banking, he had no time for corporate politics and left dealing with the MTN bureaucracy to Jonker and Van der Walt. Five months after they started back in 2012, he flicked the switch on the project, taking Mobile Money live. However, he had not told anyone it was happening. There had been no final sign-off or marketing to promote it, but curious customers discovered the USSD code on their phones and there were 10,000 registrations on the first day. They were in business, albeit suddenly.

The stories about Harms and the technology team are legion. While head office was in Rosebank, with John Kane's development lab down the road, the critical work of writing the code that made the bank function was later done from an office building in Centurion, where Harms ruled the roost and continued with his zero tolerance of outside interference with his team by anyone within CBA or the Rosebank HQ.

'I was one of the few people allowed into the building in Midrand,' says Chris Bennett, who worked for CBA at the time and later served as chief technology officer at GoTyme Bank, the joint venture in the Philippines between Tyme and the Manila-based Gokongwei Group, and he now serves as chief technology architect at the group's 600-person-strong technology hub in Ho Chi Minh City, Vietnam. He describes the relationship between the developers in Centurion and head office in Rosebank as 'dysfunctional' and was unsurprised when the team jumped ship to OUTsurance.

However, Nate Clarke, the former Deloitte US consultant who demanded to be hired when the team shifted to MTN, credits Harms' talents for securing the CBA investment in the first place. He was a rare beast in an industry where few tech leaders can deliver at speed with constrained budgets, and he had a thorough understanding of the business imperative of delivering his work: 'Ockert led the development of the Namibian bank, which is what got CBA's attention. They wouldn't have bought Tyme had he not been there.'

To build EBank, Harms created a purpose-built core banking system, which he called Prometheus. The name pleased Jonker, who interpreted it as being taken from Greek mythology where Prometheus is known for his intelligence and defiance of the gods. He is most famous for stealing fire from Olympus and giving it to humanity, an act that symbolised knowledge, progress and self-sufficiency. Scholars regard him as a champion of human ingenuity. In reality, the name was inspired by Ridley Scott's 2012 prequel to the film *Alien*, in which the ideas of creation and rebellion are explored without direct reference to the ancient myths – the joke amuses him to this day.

'CBA treated us like a "YAB" bank,' says Harms, '"Yet Another Bank". When they came in, creativity died. Not that they did anything wrong, it was just different.'

Once he and his team left, there was no one to operate Prometheus.

While his successors did what they could to maintain it, there was no documentation or other reference points for anyone not involved in developing it, so the group opted in 2017 to lease the Mambu core banking system as a service. The CBA relationship, while frustrating and often fraught, was not without considerable merits and would open doors to Southeast Asia, which the Tyme team would have found much harder to unlock independently. Jonker was building up his network and understanding the banking dynamics of multiple economies in the region, while the group deployed Nate Clarke to Indonesia to run its TymeDigital initiative, giving him his first taste of executive responsibility in a new country.

Harms' departure left Tyme in a serious bind. While it plunged the business into crisis, it was the response to the problem that later proved fortuitous. During Jonker's time as head of digital for CBA, the group had established a technology hub in Vietnam, with a focus on developing its own solutions for its businesses in Southeast Asia. The decision was made to shift development to this hub in Ho Chi Minh City – a pivotal and disruptive decision at the time, but one that would later serve the group well as it eyed new markets in the region and an independent company.

Back in South Africa, the team under CBA had been spending too much and achieving too little. Among the many issues was the fact that its cost base was too high, but the reality is the investment CBA made provided the building blocks for what the business would later become. Following Harms' departure, Tyme needed high-level tech leadership.

Dieter Botha had built banking systems within Standard Bank for a decade before he took a job with Oracle in Australia in 2014 and aspired to build a digital bank of his own. His and Jonker's paths had not crossed at Standard Bank, despite there being some overlap in the time they spent there. He did know a few people at CBA, and they suggested he help bring the Tyme project back on stream.

One day, while he was contemplating his future at his home in Sydney, his phone rang. It was Jonker inviting him for a drink and a chat. They met at De Vine Food & Wine, about a 15-minute walk from the CBA head office on the edge of Darling harbour, where Jonker made his pitch over two bottles of wine. He spelt out the vision and explained some of the problems they were facing. Costs were out of control and the project needed to be pulled together quickly. Botha would later become chief information officer and chief technical officer of the group running the team in Vietnam and developing group-wide systems.

While Tyme was struggling in South Africa, Jonker's influence at CBA was growing.

In August 2017, on the eve of it being granted a licence to operate as a fully digital bank, Patrice Motsepe's African Rainbow Capital (ARC) took a 10% stake in TymeDigital for R56 million, unaware that less than a year later it would be asked to join the founders in buying out its controlling shareholder.

For now, though, CBA was still very much on board and maintained the party line that Tyme was part of a far bigger strategy: 'We aim to build a sustainable business in South Africa,' CEO Ian Narev said, 'and to work in an open and cooperative way with the South African Reserve Bank and other relevant regulators.' He added that Tyme had the potential to become a source of research and development ideas for CBA. By this point, Sandile Shabalala had been in the job for less than a year, but he expressed equal enthusiasm: 'This is a key milestone in our plans to launch a full-service digital bank and disrupt banking in South Africa. We believe that TymeDigital will not only transform the banking landscape but will fundamentally change how South Africans consume banking products and services.'

It was the sort of bold, positive, evergreen statement kept on PR desktops to convey certainty when in fact there was none, and while Tyme faced little prospect of meeting the deadlines it had set publicly. The technology team abandoned Prometheus following a review of the code and used cloud-native Mambu to build a functioning platform on the Reserve Bank-approved Amazon Web Services in May 2018. They were still nine months away from a public launch of the offering.

There was a far bigger issue bubbling in the background that would once again threaten the very existence of Tyme. Trouble was brewing Down Under.

Narev's position as CEO of CBA had become untenable. On 14 August 2017, he announced he would resign as CEO within a year, following revelations at the Royal Commission into Misconduct in the Banking, Superannuation and Financial Services Industry. The Commission found that the banking group had breached Australian money-laundering laws 54,000 times. Two weeks previously, the Australian Transaction Reports and Analysis Centre launched civil proceedings against CBA in federal court, claiming the bank had made 'serious and systemic' violations of laws aimed at combating funding of terrorism and crime syndicates. The Australian Securities and Investments Commission said it was investigating whether CBA broke disclosure laws by not telling investors about possible money laundering by criminal gangs and suspected terrorists. The bank was also instructed to refund 65,000 customers A$10 million after mis-selling consumer credit insurance, plus it was told to refund A$586,000 in premiums to 10,000 customers after overcharging them home-loan protection insurance.

The Sydney Morning Herald commented that the outcome of the Royal Commission and the fines were a culmination of years of issues that compounded to a point where they could no longer be ignored: 'In each case the bank's default position has been to downplay issues. The financial planning scandal was brushed off as a "few bad apples", CommInsure, the bank insisted, related to a small handful of customers, even its outdated medical definitions had reasons attached, and the immediate reaction to Austrac allegations was to give briefings that it was a coding error and therefore the 53,000 breaches of the Act were really just one breach. Now we are in a situation where the bank is in crisis management. After saying on August 9 that the board had full confidence in Narev, five days later it issued a new statement offering a departure date.'[2]

Relative to its problems at home, Tyme was considerably less significant for Australia's banking behemoth, but it was a problem that needed resolving, especially considering the political and customer pressures in its home market.

In addition to its domestic troubles being painfully and publicly revealed by the Royal Commission, CBA realised that it would not achieve its target of launching the South African bank by the middle of 2018. Unless the issues were properly addressed, they might have a negative impact on CBA's plans for driving digital banking in Southeast Asia.

The disjointed build process that had so frustrated the South Africans and led to Van der Walt's exit had created dysfunctional silos in the business. CBA finally realised that not enough work had been done on the integration of disparate systems and processes. Launch was pushed out from June to September 2018 – another date the team would miss.

Keraan recalls being summoned to a 'big meeting' in Hong Kong and asked to manage the integration process and get the bank ready for launch. Shabalala was still CEO, but Keraan oversaw the engine room. By March, Keraan had a new delivery plan and a new team. He described his job as 'driving the project with intensity and joining the dots'.

The bank build was back on track. Dieter Botha had made enough of an impression on the team in Johannesburg and was appointed to head the technology division with a team in South Africa and in Vietnam. 'The base had been built by CBA, but we needed to think about it differently,' he says, 'so we started with the customer in mind, then we engaged the design team and then applied the engineering. There was a lot to do. It was bloody hard, there was a lot of trial and error, we didn't have a blueprint for what we were trying to do, so we messed up a lot.'

Narev, Tyme's most ardent supporter within CBA, left in April and his successor Matt Comyn's biggest priority was to restore the reputation of Australia's biggest and most valuable banking group. He was going to struggle to do it without focus, and getting rid of foreign assets would send the signal he needed that he was serious about doing that. Comyn had visited South Africa soon after assuming the job as CEO and appeared supportive ahead of the planned launch of the bank, still scheduled for later in the year.

However, on 25 June 2018, he announced the planned sale of CBA's non-core assets, including its non-Australian businesses. Colonial First State Global Asset Management was the first on the block, as it reviewed its broader wealth management and mortgage broking businesses. It was a key moment, signalling the bank's strategic shift. 'Colonial' was the most valuable and saleable of the businesses and the A$4-billion price tag would release welcome capital and build investor confidence. It set the stage for further divestments, including the exit from South Africa, Indonesia and China.

Jonker had already been issued with the instruction to begin sale proceedings, including finding a buyer for Tyme. This put him in a difficult position. He knew exactly what he wanted to do, but it would mean he would be an insider on both sides of a sale transaction if he could convince the stalwarts who had begun the journey with him at Standard Bank and Deloitte that they should try again.

The first meeting to test his idea was with Nate Clarke. By now, Clarke was a seasoned corporate executive who had been head of CBA's digital operations in Indonesia for about three years. He recalls meeting Jonker at a rooftop bar in Jakarta, where his boss floated the idea of taking back Tyme and once again running it themselves. They agreed that it was worth trying, acknowledging they would need outside funding and their success would depend on who would back them with as little outside interference as possible. Soon after that, they convened a meeting of about half a dozen stalwarts from the early days around the kitchen table in Jonker's home in Melville, a middle-class suburb of Johannesburg, and committed to having another go.

But who would want to buy an incomplete digital-only South African bank with no track record, which, despite having billions of rand invested in its development, was not even operational yet and kept missing its self-imposed launch dates?

Not only that, but the South African economy was on its knees, battered by industrial-scale corruption at the highest levels of government, and there was significant political instability in the country as the recently installed President Cyril Ramaphosa sought to build a power base in a divided governing party. It was going to be a hard sell. South Africa had the promise of democratic and economic revival, following more than a decade of misgovernance and the plundering of state coffers by politically connected elites, but divestment rather than investment dominated popular discussion.

The first call would need to be to ARC, which via its 10% shareholding in Tyme Group had the right of first refusal should the shareholding ever change. ARC, however, was not in the business of controlling the companies in which it invested. It had been formed with the sole purpose of taking significant minority stakes in established South African companies as part of the country's complex Black Economic Empowerment (BEE) legislation. BEE required large companies to progress black share ownership, management and participation in businesses through a complex scoring system that affected everything from government contracts, licences and even private sector deals. ARC, chaired and ultimately controlled by billionaire lawyer Patrice Motsepe, was a very attractive and in-demand partner.

But joint ARC CEO Johan van Zyl was not ready to make an offer. At the same time, if there was to be a new controlling shareholder, he would want to influence its selection, as that would have a material impact on ARC's stake.

So, on 4 July 2018, he and ARC investment executive Charmaine Padayachy made a hastily arranged trip to Hong Kong to meet the management team and potential investors. The clock was ticking. If Tyme could not find a backer in three months, Comyn warned, it would be shut down.

There were two arduous days of meetings, described as a 'beauty parade' where prospective investors were pitched the idea of the bank. The pressure to find a new investor who shared the team's vision was intense. By the end of those two days, there was just one player showing any serious interest. Standard Chartered, which had previously made a play to do retail banking in South Africa when it bought the innovative internet bank 20Twenty out of the wreckage of the Saambou Bank collapse, and saw an opportunity to use the technology stack to build a private banking operation, rather than realise the vision of a mass market bank.

They made a 'cheeky offer' that would have satisfied neither CBA nor the regulator at the South African Reserve Bank, which had issued the banking licence on the basis that it was to be a mass market offering that would seek to broaden access to banking. The regulator was open to all ideas, as it was concerned that the closure would lead to wholesale job losses. At the time, the central bank was facing significant, if misguided, pressure to be nationalised. Although governed by strict legislation and answerable to parliament through the Department of Finance, it had a legacy of private shareholders who, despite being entitled to little more than a ticket to the AGM and a civil service catered lunch once a year, were deemed by some on the hard left of South African politics to undermine what they regarded as a 'progressive agenda'. They wanted rates slashed and for the state to use the country's foreign currency reserves to bolster government spending – both actions would likely have created an inflation picture like what transpired in Turkey when the president meddled directly in the affairs of its central bank.

The noise around Reserve Bank independence was deafening and no one wanted to add fuel to the fire. With Standard Chartered deemed unsuitable, the discussion moved to a buyout by ARC and management. As a founder, Jonker was eager to rejoin the team in realising his long-held ambition to drive real financial inclusion, but, on the other hand, he was a senior executive who had been offered an enticing opportunity to join the CBA executive committee in Australia.

'There were a lot of conflicts in the mix. The conversations were very delicate,' remembers Padayachy.

As the deal was concluded, there were still various regulatory requirements that needed to be fulfilled. There was one final box to tick.

The core management team supported ARC control. Van Zyl would not have considered a deal without them. He saw the top eight members of the leadership team as the biggest asset. ARC deputy chairperson Tom Boardman, who years before had negotiated the Edward Nathan repurchase with Jonker, was concerned about the amount of capital Tyme would need – especially if it decided, as it would need to in order to be sustainable, to launch lending products.

He further warned the ARC board that there would be a significant opportunity cost, as its future deal pipeline would inevitably be restricted by the demands of the bank. His decades of banking experience had taught him some painful lessons. The country's concentrated banking sector was highly efficient and would make it very hard for a rival to compete. He also understood just how demanding the capital requirements of a bank were and questioned whether it was not too big an investment for ARC. It would be bad enough if it failed and ARC lost its money, but what if it succeeded in expanding to new markets and needed more money than its controlling shareholder could raise?

Boardman made the ARC board acutely aware of the potential consequences of investing in Tyme. 'I call it "Tom's famous speech"; he spoke for 30 minutes and scared the shit out of everyone,' laughs Van Zyl. When Boardman sat down, the mood in the boardroom was wary. The consequences of what they were being asked to consider were serious. ARC chairperson Patrice Motsepe broke the silence: 'Thank you for your wise counsel, Mr Boardman, where do I sign?'

It was the lifeline the bank needed. Had Motsepe baulked, there was no plan B. They would have been out of options. With a new cost-sensitive controlling shareholder, the work towards a launch date was under way. We warned you this story has more twists than the Monaco Grand Prix circuit.

We are barely at the first chicane.

Part IV
....

The Second Tyme

Chapter 8

The Phygital Frontier

You never change things by fighting the existing reality.
To change something, build a new model that makes the existing model obsolete.

— Buckminster Fuller

African Rainbow Capital (ARC) and the founders of Tyme received regulatory approval to buy out the Commonwealth Bank of Australia's (CBA) 90% stake on Guy Fawkes Day, 5 November 2018 – an auspicious day – but the fireworks had barely even started. They paid CBA R300 million, similar to the offer made by Standard Chartered, with one key difference – the focus would remain on financial inclusion. While ARC had the bigger financial exposure, Jonker and Van der Walt reinvested about 60% of the capital they had received when CBA bought the business in 2015 and would soon be obliged to demonstrate their faith in the business when the wheels came off the global economy during Covid.

For all the difficulties the team had with the culture CBA had brought, the Australians had invested an estimated R2 billion on system development and staff costs over that time. Tom Boardman had been placated by the amount of money that had already been spent on development and, despite the stern warning about the risks posed by banking, he realised there was an opportunity to be had.

'There was free money in the business, so we had some runway,' ARC's

CEO Johan van Zyl says. However, there were other cash-hungry investments in the ARC group, and the directors at ARC had their hands full managing their interests in up to 40 other businesses, too.

It was never a slam dunk. The South African Reserve Bank was worried that CBA was out of the picture. 'Even Coen was a bit worried,' recalls one executive, who also notes that Jonker always seemed to have a plan B in case his first idea failed. Now ARC was that plan B, and there were no other backups.

Jonker's last day as an employee of CBA was on 31 December 2018. He had turned down a lucrative pay deal and the chance to move his family to Sydney and take up an important job in a beleaguered, but critical Australian institution. 'There was never a question of walking away from Tyme,' his wife, Kerry Anderson, recalls. 'Neither of us wanted to give up on it.'

The CBA 2018 annual report announced the sale of Tyme as well as a wholesale review of its general insurance operations and confirmed the exit from multiple businesses in Australia, New Zealand and Indonesia as part of what Matt Comyn described as 'tightening our international focus, as part of the focus on becoming a simpler, better bank'.

For Tyme, the CBA era was over, but its colour scheme remained. CBA's brand was dominated by black and yellow, so its cards and corporate branding were all done in the same colours. There was no sense in changing that until it was necessary. It became apparent over time, though, as the bank expanded rapidly into the Philippines later, that the group would need to evolve to a single global brand blueprint.

At the time of writing, steps are underway to get a unified palette and a global identity as the business expands. There is broad acknowledgement that the brand positioning in South Africa could have been different at the start. Just because an offering is cost effective, it doesn't have to look cheap; it can keep its price point and reason for existence but be more aspirational.

Senior staff were given the opportunity to invest alongside ARC. Van Zyl says ARC had been willing to make up to 35% of the equity available as incentives to ensure the team moved over. The team eventually bought 30%

of the firm, tying them to the financial fortunes of the group. They had received generous payouts when CBA bought them but had seen no financial benefit beyond their salaries since. Now that they were more closely tied to their own destiny, the mood internally began to lift.

Jonker was now CEO of the Tyme Group based in Hong Kong, with Sandile Shabalala and Tauriq Keraan holding down the fort in South Africa. Tyme became the first bank in South Africa to host its entire core banking platform in the cloud – 85% of its systems were hosted by Amazon Web Services. This had a significant impact on its founding costs. It provided easy-to-access scalability, uniform security and associated cost efficiencies. And, thanks to its ambassador-led kiosks in Pick n Pay and Boxer retail outlets, there was no need for expensive bank branches.

'As regulator we had to manage both legs of the deal, first when CBA bought Tyme and later when it sold to African Rainbow Capital,' says former regulator Kuben Naidoo. 'We were quite excited, because it meant we had a majority black-owned bank for the first time in South African history.'

It came, however, with a halving of the staff complement – from about 500 people to around 250. The vast majority of those who were cut were senior executives brought on board by CBA. The Reserve Bank didn't anticipate any push-back on those cuts. Cheslyn Jacobs describes this period of rapid layoffs as the worst in his time at the bank. ARC was insistent that the business return to its philosophy of ruthless cost efficiency, and the first cost to be reduced was the headcount.

'Fintech founders need to understand unit economics at an atomic level,' says Jonker, referring also to the disagreement with South Africa's Home Affairs minister over the cost of ID verification. Even changing one element of the model can be enough to challenge the viability of an entire product set.

The group had lost its way during the CBA era, but financial restraint and reducing the frictional cost of doing business were once again a core focus as they built leaner, more focused teams in South Africa and Vietnam, where Dieter Botha was building a team of developers to help realise the vision of being a multi-country digital bank.

PART IV: THE SECOND TYME

After a low-key launch to the industry in November 2018, the team was confident that Tyme Bank was finally fit for public consumption. It launched its South African offering to customers in February 2019, with an EveryDay transactional account bundled with a unique savings tool called GoalSave, its SendMoney solution and its TymeCoach app, which gave customers free access to their credit report, as well as tips on better money management.

The systems were up and operational and working as they should – between the kiosks at Home Affairs and the credit bureaus, as well as between its cloud hosting service and the bank's various digital platforms. It had 500 operational kiosks on launch day and orders for 230 more to ensure an even distribution across Pick n Pay and Boxer stores, with 14,000 till points where customers could transact.

John Kane's Tyme machines weren't working optimally. They were about as simple as they could be. The earliest models were not particularly robust, using an android tablet as a screen, connected via a mobile modem to the internet, with a tabletop card printer installed to dispense a personalised debit card. They were fast and cheap to build, but they were not of industrial quality, having been designed and built by a team whose core business was in the creation of sets for the movie business. There were lots of glitches. Ambassadors used 30-centimetre plastic school rulers to realign stuck cards in the machines. It was not a good look.

'There was no guidebook on what we were trying to achieve,' says chief risk officer at TymeBank Owen Sorour. Also previously from Standard Bank, he had joined Tyme because, like so many others, he wanted to be close to the centre of building something new, rather than being one of hundreds of cogs in a large company machine. 'It was all about making the best next decision,' he says about the trial-and-error approach the bank embarked on as it sought new opportunities. 'We just had to ensure that we limited the blast radius of the damage when things did go wrong. The good thing about going to war with the right people, and everyone multi-skilling all the time, is that you eventually sort out problems.'

The devices that were connected to an unreliable government mainframe at the Department of Home Affairs were not immune to breakdowns.

Cards that should have been seamlessly issued by the machine would regularly get stuck and failure rates were high, especially since rapid customer acquisition was a core focus for the group. In addition, they also needed to improve the value of transactions per customer. It was pointless getting them to sign up and the accounts going dormant or only used for a once-a-month cash withdrawal after payday. The existing banks were responding to the new player aggressively by upping their own digital capabilities and trimming fees to disincentivise a move to the upstart.

Dietmar Böhmer studied mathematics and actuarial science and spent some time in academia. He anticipated joining a big insurer but found himself in banking instead and joined Tyme when CBA took over. His job was to better understand the growing customer base. The efficiency of the bank relies on identifying any bottlenecks in processing to minimise friction for customers who increasingly demand the ability to transact digitally in an instant.

'We measure and track exactly what happens on each and every screen. What do people do? How long are they on the screen? What buttons do they press? Obviously, on some screens, if you spend much more time here than others, maybe there's something that's confusing here, or people aren't sure what to do next,' he explains. In a world where service models increasingly look to reduce human intervention, ensuring that a platform is intuitive and easily accessible is vital.

'We use fancy terms like gen AI and machine analytics and testing systems and processes and all that sort of stuff, but in practice the job is all about data and creating a single view of the customer,' says Böhmer. The group's ability to automate loan applications relies on more than just a clean credit score from a third-party provider. Every action a customer takes online helps Böhmer construct a picture of their likely ability to pay back a loan. His team monitors customer activity constantly, looking for usage patterns and, critically, changes in behaviour that contribute to a fuller understanding of their financial circumstances, which enables the group to make better-quality lending decisions.

'It's all about continuous improvement, continuous monitoring and really obsessing about that customer experience,' says Böhmer. In those early days, there was a lot to fix.

'You have to be comfortable with failure,' says Botha, a technologist who has a philosophy of speedy development and being willing 'to fix the plane while it's flying'. This is the antithesis of what young Vietnamese are taught at school, where failure is frowned upon in a country striving for growth. To inject a culture of greater risk-taking, Botha introduced monthly awards at the Vietnam tech hub to encourage risk-taking in the creative process of developing complex systems to run the banking operations. He recognised that the young developers coming out of the local education system were reticent to push the boundaries and were averse to failure. So he began publicly acknowledging the courage of those who dared to push the boundaries and make mistakes as a result. They knew that their risk appetite set the boundaries of their potential development: too tight and they moved too slowly, too loose and they risked making too many expensive mistakes that took time to resolve.

'Good risk management is about allowing an issue to surface, be managed and worked through without recrimination for individuals,' says chief risk officer at GoTyme in the Philippines, Josam Watson. Global standards on risk-taking emerged following the global financial crisis and, despite its very public failings, CBA had imposed a culture of 'risk elimination' rather than a more fluid risk management process, and that had led to an internal audit function in the business of about 60 people by the time the Australians sold out. By comparison, the group now has a team of six.

'It's very different from the CBA days,' Watson says. 'We have introduced a philosophy of "risk is everyone's business", which means that there is individual accountability rather than the time-consuming compromises that emerge from committees.' There are, of course, overall guardrails, clear delegation of authority and documented boundaries that draw on global best practice, borrowed from the best regulatory frameworks in the world, including South Africa, which has built up a solid international reputation in bank supervision this century. It is a process of exposing and resolving issues as they arise, rather than getting caught up in the messy politics of blame, finger-pointing and recrimination.

'That first year with ARC was chaotic,' recalls Nate Clarke. 'It was euphoric, naive and sometimes stupid,' he says, remembering the pace of development and exploration of potential new markets. The team was obsessed with making up for lost time. The result was a rapid cash burn without a commensurate increase in revenue from their activities. While they were signing up customers in record numbers, too few of the millions of newly acquired customers on their books were transacting often enough to justify the expense of serving them.

They looked for new opportunities in markets where large numbers of people were outside of an inefficient financial system and which had progressive regulators eager to drive inclusion. Van der Walt was back in the business – he was seen as the calm stable influence in the background, ensuring that the tracks were in place, which allowed for the high-speed train in Jonker to pursue growth opportunities.

Countries needed a national ID card system that enabled the team to verify the identity of their customers. The target countries needed networks of large established retailers with national reach, where they could house their Tyme machines and gain access to their customers. Regulations had to allow fully cloud-based, offshore, hardware solutions. Plus, they were unwavering on Van der Walt's key principles – there could be no physical paperwork to create friction in the application and approval process, and nobody associated with Tyme should handle cash.

All these principles were designed to allow Tyme to create sustainable, profitable businesses within a reasonable time frame, believed to be between three and five years from launch. These needs narrowed their options quickly, as they found stumbling blocks in markets like Egypt and Pakistan, where one or more of their requirements would not be met in any reasonable time frame. Rather than spend valuable time and limited resources trying to mould the environment to their needs, they needed to focus on where they could get started without having to navigate complex domestic issues.

They came close to launching in Malaysia, where all the stars appeared to align. Watson recalls his best day at Tyme as being the day they opted to not enter that country, despite it being an appealing market. It was all systems go; they had local partners lined up, and everything about making it the next market for the group made sense. One week before they were about to make their final application, they noticed a single clause in the domestic banking regulation that would have altered their capital requirements from the third year of their starting up. Being forced to hold additional capital would have a devastating impact on their ability to make a return and delayed break-even from three years to nine years. On that basis, it did not meet the investment case and Tyme withdrew. It had taken money and valuable management time, but the group took comfort from the fact that they had stood firm and stuck to the core investment principles.

Back in South Africa, they were signing up thousands of new customers a day, which meant they were burning through cash. The irony was that the faster they grew and signed up customers, the more they spent without a matching increase in revenues. Many of those joining the bank had not had an account before and, although charges were kept low compared to their peers, any fee represented a reduction in the amount of money they had to spend.

Long before Covid and its first ill-fated lending product was launched, Tyme had realised that to be profitable and expand, it needed to get into the lending business. The first conversations about a possible tie-up between Jonker and Retail Capital founder and CEO Karl Westvig started before Covid. They liked each other and respected one another's businesses, but the timing wasn't yet right to send out wedding invitations. That would come later.

Westvig began his career in retail in the mid-1990s, honing his expertise in a rapidly evolving market. With a Business Science degree and a strong foundation in statistics, he developed an early fascination with lending models for lower-income customers. It was a time of minimal regulation and significant market flexibility, creating opportunities for innovation. By 1997, he had co-founded Direct Axis with funding from Boland Bank to build an outbound call-centre-based lending platform. The business leveraged batch scoring, a method of assessing creditworthiness by analysing groups of applicants rather than individuals in real-time, allowing for more efficient and scalable loan approvals. The founders sold it within two years and followed it with the RCS Group, which they later sold to investors, including Standard Bank. Westvig left there in 2003, soon after the imposition of the National Credit Act, which started to put a cap on rates lenders could levy on loans.

He took a break and went travelling. On his return, he launched five businesses, teaching him the lesson of his life – focus. 'No matter how smart you think you are, it's draining, and they all end up needing capital at the same time,' says Westvig. So, in early 2011, he homed in on one business concept that originated in the US and came to South Africa via the UK. It lent money to small businesses based on their cash flow. It was flexible enough to collect only when the company that had borrowed the money traded and, when it did, Retail Capital was able to harvest a percentage of the daily turnover until its debt was settled. He first became aware of Jonker and the early version of what would become Tyme in 2012. In late 2019, he started talking to Jonker about a possible tie-up, but the deal made no sense to him. He was not about to swap shares in his profitable lending business to take up shares in an unprofitable retail bank.

When the lockdowns hit in early 2020, Westvig took defensive steps, drawing money from every facility the company had to provide liquidity for what he assumed would be an extended period. He cut operating costs by a third to R8 million a month and had enough to last up to eight months if he was not able to collect a single cent.

In April, with a book of R85 million, he was able to collect R12 million. It wasn't much, but it was something, and he opened communications with investors, lenders and customers – transparency, he believed, would help him weather the uncertainty. He continued lending through the cycle, but only from money he had managed to collect, and he kept the wheels of the business turning until markets started to open again.

The next time the pair would meet was in February 2022. Jonker was about to be announced as CEO once again of the South African business, and they chatted over coffee at the landmark Vineyard Hotel in Cape Town, agreeing in principle that a tie-up made sense. Within weeks, they had a structure that would see Retail Capital subsumed by Tyme over two years. It was a complex deal that was finalised only in July and finally approved in December.

Retail Capital was ring-fenced, and they developed reporting lines. They worked together for a year as Westvig bedded down the business now as a division of Tyme, but at the end of December 2023 Jonker and Westvig met up again.

Westvig committed to spending between 18 and 36 months, but Jonker, ever looking to maximise the skills and talents of those around him, asked him about his intentions. Did he want to be all in or all out? After all, Jonker was doing three demanding jobs simultaneously; Group, South Africa and expansion projects, plus he still somehow had to travel back to Singapore occasionally to see his family. Westvig describes himself as a 'reluctant CEO' but accepted the role to free up the founder to pursue new opportunities.

For retail banking to work at scale, it needs lots of customers having income regularly deposited into their account and transacting often. You also want them borrowing money from you and paying you back as per the agreed terms, ensuring you not only recoup your capital but are rewarded with an interest payment for taking on the risk of the loan. That is easier said than done. It's a competitive landscape, in which the incumbents have the advantage of deep market penetration, brand recognition and the trust earned by the fact that they have survived as long as they have. As a startup, you can provide better service, a better user experience and a better deal, but if your customers don't know who you are, they are likely to be circumspect in trusting you with their money. Brand recognition is vital in building that trust. A quote commonly attributed to the pioneering American merchant and marketing innovator at the turn of the 19th century, John Wanamaker, encapsulates the problem perfectly for budget-conscious startups: 'Half the money I spend on advertising is wasted; the trouble is I don't know which half.'

As Tyme launched and secured its banking licence, Cheslyn Jacobs was struggling to contain himself. He sought creative new ways to draw attention to the offering and was unencumbered by a sense of decorum that is traditionally observed by the industry. Some of Tyme's early marketing efforts riled its opponents. Tyme put up a billboard on Oxford Road, facing the Standard Bank head office. It read: 'WHY SHOULD BANKING BE STANDARD?' with an 11% Tyme interest rate offer for deposits pasted underneath, and with another slight: 'Tyme to move on.' Other billboards mocking FNB were erected on highways, using a shade of blue indecently close to that of the bank, which had previously been named as most innovative in the world, with the line: 'Money doesn't grow on trees', a clear swipe at FNB's thorn tree logo. It was cheeky, irreverent and created plenty of social media chatter. It also upset the incumbents. Jacobs, however, was looking for attention, and he got it.

'I asked him to tone it down a bit,' smiles Jonker, recalling donning a tie to visit Standard Bank to apologise to his old boss, Sim Tshabalala, for his colleague's behaviour. His apology was genuine – he has great respect for Tshabalala; besides, he was also in no position to go to war with deep-pocketed incumbents. At the same time, he was proud of the terrier-like energy of his team for growth. That boded well for the future.

Chapter 9

217 Calls, the Pawnshop King and the Ticking Time Bomb

> Calvin: 'Know what I pray for? The strength to change what I can, the inability to accept what I can't, and the incapacity to tell the difference.'
> Hobbs: 'You should lead an interesting life.'
> — Bill Watterson

In the last week of February 2019, TymeBank launched to the public. By the middle of 2019, African Rainbow Capital (ARC) and Ethos Private Equity jointly announced an investment of R200 million by the Ethos AI Fund and co-investors in Tyme. Ethos now had an 8% stake in the business. The pressure was real. Sandile Shabalala packed his bags in August and into the breach stepped Tauriq Keraan as CEO.

Three months later, Tyme celebrated signing up its one-millionth customer. It was competing aggressively on price, as well as paying a premium to attract deposits. It provocatively published like-for-like fees in official documents and presented these to parliament as part of its value proposition. It published its comparative staffing numbers: 250 permanent and 555 contract staff mostly managing the kiosks, while its retail partnerships meant it had the second highest number of points of presence after juggernaut Capitec. Standard Bank had the biggest headcount with some 48,000 staff, followed by FNB and Absa, which both had more than 40,000 staff. The incumbents were reducing branch numbers to lower costs, while Capitec maintained a strong physical presence in the market. To be fair, Tyme's product suite was considerably smaller than its established rivals – but what the market saw, it liked.

By the end of its first year, nearly half its customers were digitally savvy over-35-year-olds, two-thirds earned up to R5,000 a month (equivalent to about US$300 at the time), while about one-third earned more than that.

The problem with growth is that when things go wrong, they go spectacularly wrong at scale. The new bank faced its first real test in December 2019, when South Africa is traditionally on its summer holidays and spending over bank systems goes into overdrive. It was during this time that Tyme experienced a catastrophic outage. Ambassadors on the ground were powerless to placate customers who could not access cash, nor transact on their debit cards. Tempers frayed. Staff were threatened and, in some cases, customers refused to leave retail stores, demanding to know where their money was. As a new player in the market, Tyme had little brand equity, and it was a reminder that they needed to do better.

As the second decade of the 21st century ended – nearly 20 years after Jonker's light-bulb moment in a classroom at GIBS in Illovo ignited an idea that was finally poised for take-off – no one could have foreseen that the year ahead would become its *annus horribilis*. The business was about to face an existential crisis that would test its very survival.

As 2020 dawned, the years of experimentation, investment, hope, heartache and hard knocks had finally coalesced and Tyme was growing customer numbers and its deposit base. It had a dependable shareholder that left a management team it trusted, ready to lend. The lending product was in the market, the bank's systems had been stabilised, and they were three weeks away from closing their latest capital raise.

Things were finally looking up.

'My advice when they decided to launch the loan product was to proceed very cautiously,' says Tom Boardman. 'Whenever there is a new entrant into a loan market, whether it is for mortgages or at the lower end, there is this negative selection in that it attracts all the people who have not been able to get credit anywhere else. If the big names haven't given the credit, it is usually for a good reason, so when you are a new entrant, it is your most risky and dangerous time in terms of bad debts.'

There was an exciting new growth opportunity, and the group had focused its collective energy preparing for an Easter launch to one of the most sought-after communities in the country – the 10-million-strong Zion Christian Church (ZCC). Patrice Motsepe had made good on his promise to make an introduction to the Church, which had tried and failed for years to create a dedicated banking offering with the country's large banks.

Tyme was to offer ZCC members a Zion City Moria membership card. It would not only demonstrate their Church affiliation, but its functionality would allow speedier access to mass events at the group's base in the country's Limpopo Province and work as a bank card that would be distributed through the Church using specially built mobile Tyme machines. Motsepe was adept at big launches.

When he led the BEE deal with Sanlam in the early 2000s, Motsepe ensured that real-life beneficiaries of the trusts that invested in the life insurer converged on the Hilton hotel in Sandton. It was a festive atmosphere to signal that the deal he had brokered would have broader reach than hundreds of others that were criticised for only growing the wealth of a few politically connected individuals. He used the same playbook to amplify the ZZC tie-up with Tyme. Church members arrived at the Church's spiritual home at Moria in about 100 buses. Motsepe was there with Johan van Zyl and ZCC's Bishop Barnabas Lekganyane. The machine failed. It took four attempts to issue the bishop with a personalised card. Motsepe, according to eyewitnesses, was displeased.

Manufacture of the kiosks soon shifted to a proper industrial manufacturer in Taiwan and subsequent launches were less fraught. When the first card was publicly issued to JG Summit Holdings CEO Lance Gokongwei at the Philippines launch of GoTyme, it worked first time. There is a picture of Chris Bennett joyfully punching the air with both fists, relieved that they had avoided a repeat performance of the near debacle in the African bushveld.

Within weeks of the ZCC launch, South Africa went into hard lockdown. The Church never fully endorsed the product and fewer than 200,000 people signed up. And as far as its promising lending product was concerned, it would barely be in the market long enough to face that problem and would soon have far bigger issues to deal with.

In February 2020, all was proceeding to plan, and it was as a good an opportunity as any, thought Coen Jonker, to escort his oldest daughter, Cailen, to Peru, where she intended working in a relative's guest house and travelling as part of a gap year preceding her psychology studies.

Since the middle of January, there had been worrying signals of a virus emerging in Wuhan in China that appeared to be spreading quickly around the globe. On 28 February, the World Health Organization warned that global risk levels were very high and that efforts to contain its spread were failing. A week earlier, the Italian government had imposed a lockdown in 11 municipalities in Lombardy and Veneto, affecting 50,000 people. By 8 March, 14 other northern Italian provinces were in full lockdown, and the next day the entire country became the first in Europe to order its citizens to remain at home.

On 9 March, the Dow Jones Industrial Average fell 2,013 points, nearly 8% – its single biggest ever one-day points drop in history, wiping out nearly US$2 trillion in value. Brent Crude oil prices plunged to $31 a barrel as Saudi Arabia announced a massive price cut following failed OPEC+ talks with Russia. The value of energy companies plummeted as markets anticipated a collapse in demand for fuel and as more and more lockdowns loomed. There were further massive sell-offs as lockdowns spread across the globe and fear gripped markets.

It is hardly surprising, therefore, that credit markets and private equity were being strangled. Corporate bond yields spiked, and investors dumped riskier corporate debt, leading to soaring yields, particularly in high-yield or junk bonds. Liquidity dried up and companies suddenly struggled to issue new debt. Investors raced into the perceived safety of US Treasuries, which caused yields to plunge to record lows. The ten-year Treasury fell below 1% for the first time ever on 9 March. Naturally, deal-making ground to a halt. Fundraising collapsed and the ability to exit investments stalled as the market froze.

Despite this, Jonker and his daughter continued their journey to the small town of Huaran in Peru's majestic Sacred Valley, located between Calca and Urubamba – an area not far from the famed Machu Picchu, known for its Inca ruins and spectacular ancient agricultural terraces.

No sooner had they arrived than Jonker began relooking at his travel options. He needed to get back to Hong Kong in a hurry. Large parts of the world were shutting down and travel was becoming increasingly difficult. He managed to secure a flight out of Peru on 16 March. But the day before, President Martín Vizcarra ordered the first national shutdown in Latin America, which closed all borders, introduced mandatory curfews, internal travel restrictions and the suspension of non-essential business activity.

Two days later, the lead investor in Tyme's critical US$100-million Series B capital raise announced they were withdrawing and within days the rest followed. The firm was back in deep crisis, with its group CEO stuck in Peru and any semblance of stability Jonker had enjoyed just weeks before evaporated. Tyme was back in survival mode.

The firm once again went into overdrive to reduce its R100-million-per-month cash burn. It shut down its loan product within days of its launch and, rather than go through more layoffs, all staff took salary cuts. The shareholders dug painfully into their own pockets for what Jonker describes as a 'small funding round'. He, Tjaart van der Walt, ARC and Ian Narev followed their rights at the same pricing that the Series B had been levelled at to ensure business continuity.

It demonstrated high conviction at probably the most irrational point in the history of the business, as there was no time frame as to how long countries would remain locked down and how long it would take for confidence to return to markets and eventually to consumers. Without that conviction, Tyme would have become a casualty of Covid. For now, at least, with careful cost management, they had sufficient cash, they hoped, to see them through to the end of the year.

While Jonker busied himself on managing the immediate crisis, he handed over the problem of getting back home to Hong Kong from Peru to his assistant, Jenny Chan. There were no commercial flights and borders were heavily policed. Gradually, however, governments realised they would have to find ways to repatriate citizens. The pandemic was going to restrict human movement for many months, not the 'few weeks' that the first optimistic forecasts had suggested. Thus was born a complex global system of flights and in-country quarantines that allowed limited travel to take place with strict health precautions.

It took five weeks for a plan to be made, during which time Jonker worked through the nights in Peru to manage the complexity of multiple time zones the business needed to cover. With the help of Jeremy Tan, a pro-democracy lawmaker in Hong Kong's Legislative Council, Jenny Chan had managed to secure a spot for Jonker to join a group of elderly Thai Chi practitioners who had been on a cultural tour to Peru, when they, too, had been trapped by the shutdowns.

Jonker would need to get to the town of Cusco, some three hours away. While his passage out of the country was secured, there was no guarantee that he would be able to make it through the mountains without running into trouble at what transpired to be eight police roadblocks along the way. A 'friend of a friend' was a policeman who offered to drive him. He had the correct documentation to make the journey to Cusco, but there was strong anti-foreigner sentiment in the country at the time and no guarantee that an overzealous official might not cause a delay or, worse, throw him in a jail cell for an indefinite period. He could not risk missing the flight to Hong Kong, as there was no assurance of when the next opportunity might arise.

He decided the best course of action would be to fold his six-foot frame into the boot of a Toyota RAV4 and began the long journey over rough, winding mountain roads to meet up with the Tai Chi squad. The vehicle was waved through seven of the checkpoints. At the eighth checkpoint, the boot was briefly opened. There was a moment that resembled the high drama of a John le Carré novel as Jonker lay beneath a pile of fabric, waiting to be dragged out and thrown in jail. Only a cursory examination was made and, with his heart pounding loudly, the pair continued on their way.

PART IV: THE SECOND TYME

With a couple of days to go before the flight left Cusco – via Lima and onwards to Hong Kong – the local police made their rounds at the hotel. If they happened to spot a lanky, clearly non-Chinese man, standing a full head taller than everyone else and looking more 'flailing scarecrow' than 'serene Tai Chi master', they chose not to ask questions.

Back in Hong Kong, Jonker began the first of what would become several three-week quarantine stints in box-like designated hotel rooms, spending his days on calls with his team, potential investors and an increasingly worried Johan van Zyl, weighing up the future of the business. ARC couldn't keep pouring money into it. It was leveraged against Sanlam shares, which had started the year at R80 but had nearly halved by the end of the first quarter, putting their bank covenants at risk.

Tyme chief analytics officer Dietmar Böhmer had moved from South Africa to Hong Kong in the six months before Covid hit. His team, which comprises a mix of AI specialists, data scientists, business intelligence analysts, management information specialists and data engineers, was painting a grim picture of the company's precarious position. 'I've got two crowns and two implants, which was just from that stress at night, when even with a bite guard I literally broke teeth from grinding them together. We got to a point when we had just six weeks of money – it was desperate.'

He estimates Jonker made more than 200 investor calls in the six months between his return to Hong Kong in April and October. 'I spoke to everyone we could think of,' recalls Jonker. He reddens at the memory of the persistent rejections that flowed daily: 'It was traumatic.' In the background, Van Zyl was equally desperate and began to consider his options. Boardman's warning about the risk of investing in banks was ringing in his ears as he faced up to the possibility of a worst-case scenario, where new funding could not be raised and, rather than jeopardise the rest of the portfolio, ARC might need to pull the plug.

Jonker was relentless in his efforts to secure funding. An impact investment firm called LeapFrog examined its options on Tyme half a dozen times – it became labelled internally as 'the frog that doesn't leap'. They sought funding from state institutions in South Africa, including the Public

Investment Corporation, and were prepared to cede control – to no avail. They were so desperate they even made themselves available to investment from South African banks and telcos, including Standard Bank and Vodacom, but they had no takers.

By July 2020, the pressure was becoming unbearable, and shareholders were seriously questioning whether Jonker was the right person for the job. The business needed new shareholders, but no one was biting. If Jonker was unable to convince investors to back the business, they would need to find someone who could. It wasn't the business model or the management team, but rather the fact that South Africa was deemed to be uninvestible at this time. Its tough lockdown regime meant there was no signal as to when the country, which had to wait its turn to get vaccines, would return to anything resembling 'business as usual' – whatever that would mean in a post-Covid world. Something had to give.

'We needed someone who could raise capital and Coen wasn't doing that,' says Van Zyl. 'It was never a question of his individual commitment, but we were concerned.' A group of minority shareholders believed Jonker was too loyal to his team and began discussing alternative strategies. It was time, they felt, for Jonker to hand over to someone with a more successful track record in raising funding.

Van Zyl was introduced to three people and settled on former New Zealand hockey Olympian Stuart Grimshaw, who had represented the country at the 1984 Olympics. He had a storied career in Australian banking, spending eight years at Commonwealth Bank of Australia and National Australia Bank, with stints at Yorkshire Bank and Clydesdale Bank in the UK. He had had a brief stint at the Bank of Queensland, overseeing a period of impressive growth before joining Nasdaq-listed EZCORP, a prominent US-based pawn-shop franchise, as executive chairperson in 2014. He became its CEO in 2015, based in New York, and, as Tyme went through its numerous travails, was open to a new opportunity.

Jonker was instructed to draw up an offer for his successor and bring him up to speed. He agreed. Not doing so would have limited his options. He knew that if he could raise the capital needed to dig Tyme out of the crisis

PART IV: THE SECOND TYME

he might just be able to get shareholders back on his side and get them to withdraw the offer to Grimshaw.

'Coen was amazing through this process, considering that the shareholders were looking to helicopter someone else in to replace him. He spent many weekends with Stuart, talking him through the business and ensuring that key members of his team brought him up to speed as well,' says ARC's Charmaine Padayachy.

It was no one's fault that the pandemic had upended all of their best-laid plans – but there would be a point when perpetual support of a dying business would negatively impact on others in the portfolio. There was no denying the mess they were in, and they understood ARC's legitimate concerns. Since the acquisition, ARC had put about R1.5 billion into the business. Van Zyl and his co-CEO, Johan van der Merwe, had put some of their own money into Tyme, and its perpetual ongoing losses were hurting them personally. Time was running out for Jonker to prove his value, and it became clear that the controlling shareholder was poised to announce the leadership change.

At this point, battle-weary Jonker started doubting whether it was worth reversing the decision to hire Grimshaw. But Nate Clarke, known in the team for his extreme and sometimes annoying persistence, would not accept that. After one of his onboarding sessions with Grimshaw, he drafted a list of reasons why the change would not work and phoned Padayachy, warning he would resign and that the others would also leave should the Grimshaw appointment be confirmed. Clarke recalls her being supportive and sometimes finishing his sentences as he brought up points against the new appointment.

To call it brinkmanship would be too strong, but it certainly was an unequivocal warning to the controlling shareholder, which had invested in Tyme based on the quality of the team, that any rash move would have serious consequences.

Padayachy, who had been working closely with the Tyme team since 2018 and had participated in raising capital alongside the beleaguered CEO, felt strongly that her firm was about to make a damaging judgement call. She now questions the rationality of her intervention at the time, but her gut instinct told her Grimshaw was not the right person at that point to take over from Jonker. He simply did not have the depth of experience, nor was the culture fit right.

'If anything, the business desperately needed Coen at this time,' she says.

Tense days followed, with multiple meetings inside ARC and between it, Jonker and the leadership team. The business had reached a tipping point, and the decisions that would follow in the hours and days ahead would determine the fate of the entire group. She felt the time had come to have a full and frank discussion with her boss – to not do so would have betrayed her fundamental belief that the entire future of the bank hinged on this one single call.

'It may not ever have counted for anything, but I owed it to myself to speak up,' she says. 'I told him I did not believe that it was the right way to treat Coen or the management team, that I did not believe Grimshaw was the correct appointment, and if a new CEO was needed, it should be done with the support of the leadership team.' It was a tough discussion. 'We had a leadership team that was about to walk, and ARC might lose its entire investment.'

Van Zyl paused. Then came not one but two eleventh-hour breakthroughs.

Stock markets had begun their recovery in the second quarter of 2020, as hopes rose for speedy vaccine roll-outs, which would eventually lead to a gradual opening of the global economy. Central banks had cut interest rates to the bone, and many government bonds were already yielding negative returns. This meant that investors were paying for the privilege of holding those assets, and they would receive less money than they had initially invested if they held them to maturity. At some point, the risk appetite had to return.

It may have been luck, serendipity or the result of sheer bloody-minded determination and the ability to withstand persistent rejection, but two things happened in quick succession that changed everything. A bit like the old tale that you can wait hours for a London bus, only to have two turn up at the same time, suddenly two investors agreed independently of one another to put fresh capital into the ailing startup.

PART IV: THE SECOND TYME

Nic Smalle had first met Van der Walt when he was managing the Old Mutual Strategic Investment fund, when the team was working on Project Ubiquity at MTN. 'I remember thinking it sounds insane, but we were seeing lots of other companies at the time, and I thought nothing more about it,' says Smalle.

Six years later, the opportunity presented itself once again. This time he was at Apis, a private equity firm specialising in investing in fast-growing companies in Africa, South and Southeast Asia. The idea of a multi-country digital bank appealed to him, and the low-cost proposition made sense, particularly in South Africa where large banks with their big cost centres were finding it impossible to cut bank charges in a meaningful way. He committed to invest as part of a refreshed Series B capital round.

Just days later came the breakthrough the team had been working on for months – access to the rapidly growing Philippine economy. JG Summit Holdings was headed by Lance Gokongwei, and he was looking to put his mark on the family business following the death of his father.

The Philippines deal had been in the wings for months. Rachel Freeman, who had previously worked at the International Finance Corporation, which is part of the World Bank, is a consummate networker and connector of influential people in Southeast Asia. She had spent her career building meaningful relationships across public and private sectors in anything to do with financial services, and her connections were about to hand Tyme the opportunity it needed to prove the ubiquity of the Tyme model.

She had been looking for opportunities in different countries in Southeast Asia for months. Vietnam had potential, Indonesia was ripe for disruption, but a call from Varun Mittal put paid to that idea. Mittal styled himself as a fintech matchmaker. He had written the book *Singapore: The Fintech Nation*, charting Singapore's strategic choices it had taken to become a centre of excellence in the region for financial technology.

In addition to his day job, Mittal is a passionate ambassador for the fintech explosion in the region. It is precisely that environment that had drawn Tyme to move its headquarters to the island state in the first place. He made a call to Freeman: 'The Philippines is opening new banking licences in two weeks; you need to talk to the families.'

Freeman had been doing her research in anticipation of this moment and knew there were a handful of families with the right profile who owned the supermarkets Tyme needed to house its kiosks.

Covid travel restrictions were still in place, so connecting with the families digitally saved a considerable amount of travel and avoided the need for extended one-on-one meetings. Freeman began setting up a series of meetings with the country's wealthiest families to assess their appetite to partner with a fledgling digital bank they had never heard of, which came from a country with deep political, social and economic fractures.

Freeman had mapped out her strategy and held two calls a day over a ten-day period with key figures in the Philippines, leaving her preferred partner for last, knowing full well that by the time their appointment happened, Lance Gokongwei would have got wind of Tyme's intentions. She gained access to Gokongwei via a contact in Cambodia by the name of Jojo Malolos, as well as an introduction via the global advisory firm Rothschild. Networks matter.

They set up a call. Thirty minutes into the conversation, Gokongwei demonstrated his enthusiasm: 'I am available to spend more time to discuss building a bank in the Philippines.' He was taken by the model and could see the benefit of the kiosks positioned inside his stores. They reached an in-principle agreement.

Jonker, famed for the persuasive power of his pitches, presented the big idea to the man who would become a significant investor. The bank in the Philippines would be branded GoTyme, in part, at least, as a homage to his prospective new business partner's family name and part great marketing that would position the brand as aspirational among younger people. Together, Apis and JG Summit Holdings committed US$110 million. That would be followed in 2021 by investment firm CDC (now British International Investments) and Chinese tech behemoth Tencent, part-owned, coincidentally, by South African listed tech and media company Naspers, which added another US$70 million to the pot. Van Zyl relented.

Jonker could stay, but he would need to inform Grimshaw that his services would not be required.

A press release at the time quoted Motsepe as saying: 'The ability to attract investors of this calibre is a testament to the global competitiveness of Tyme's value proposition, and its management.' At that point, no one outside a small group of insiders knew just how close they had come to the brink.

It had been the corporate equivalent of a classic Mexican standoff, the kind you would see in old cowboy films – three armed men in a triangle, each aiming at the others, knowing that if one shoots, they may all fall. Although the term is dated now, it still captures a situation where no party can advance or retreat without significant cost – so everyone remains locked in place.

Five years on, Jonker is characteristically reflective about that time: 'I wanted to understand why one of the shareholders who pushed for my replacement as CEO thought I needed to go. He told me that in times of crisis, like Covid, companies need leaders who are prepared to "pry the last dollar from the hands of a dying baby". He meant it as a joke, but it revealed something I only recognised later about the psychology of crisis: the deeply held and rarely examined belief that survival demands extreme self-interest.'

That same shareholder later said something else to Jonker that clarified where the fault lines lay in the power struggle.

'I spoke to him about "our team", meaning our colleagues at Tyme,' Jonker recalls. 'He stopped me and said, "Those people are not your team. You are a shareholder. Your shareholders are your team."'

It exposed the growing disconnect that can emerge between operators and investors in tough times. Founders often remain anchored in the purpose that inspired them to build the business, while investors – having put capital at risk – become increasingly focused on returns. At best, this creates a productive tension: investors push for disciplined financial performance; founders remind them what made the business worth building in the first place.

But in this case, the investors weren't interested in balance. They saw an opportunity to install leadership with a more hard-edged approach – one that prioritised aggressive returns over the founding philosophy. That philosophy had always been to prove that a bank could be both profitable and socially transformative: offering sustainable access to financial services to people long excluded by legacy institutions that deemed them 'unbankable'.

'To my mind,' Jonker reflects, 'the purpose of business is to serve – to create value for society and, if possible, to change the world for the better. Profit is both a self-correcting measure – proof that we are offering good value – and a way to attract capital in support of our purpose. Shareholder wealth is a fortunate by-product of a successful business, not the reason it exists. One might survive by doing what that shareholder suggested. But it hardly seems a life worth living.'

'Coen strikes me as a guy who's always got a plan B, so while he was being nice to Stuart and introducing Stuart, he was peddling like a maniac to bring investors on board,' says Padayachy. Apis and JG Summit invested in February 2021, and Tencent and CDC in December 2021.

With new investors on board, Van Zyl also had breathing room. He had recouped the money ARC had invested in Tyme – as far as he was concerned, he had derisked the investment – and any further returns would be welcome upside. The entry of new investors towards the end of 2020 brought the reinforcement ARC needed to maintain its controlling stake. 'When big international investors come in and they do a thorough due diligence and they invest, then you kind of say, well, maybe we aren't that stupid,' says Boardman.

While the funding from Apis was critical, it was signing a deal with JG Summit Holdings that would be a game changer – marking a step-change for the business as it became Tyme's first foreign foray as an independent entity. If the model that had been so effective in South Africa could be replicated in the Philippines, it seemed logical that it could be applied elsewhere.

Chapter 10

Building the Tyme Machine

Becoming is better than being. No matter what your ability is, effort is what ignites that ability and turns it into accomplishment.
— Carol Dweck

Branch banking: Built to last, priced to fail

The branch banking model took off in the late 19th and early 20th centuries. Britain, Canada, Australia, India, France, Germany and Japan were early movers in embracing nationwide branching, allowing banks to open in numerous locations.

Canada's adoption of the branch model was necessitated by its vast geography and small, dispersed population, leading banks like the Bank of Montreal (1817), Toronto-Dominion Bank (1855) and Royal Bank of Canada (1864) to establish widespread networks. In Britain, the need to support industrialisation and trade expansion saw the likes of the Bank of Scotland (1695), Lloyds Bank (1765) and Midland Bank (1836) build extensive branch operations from the late 18th century. Australia's rapid economic growth during the gold-rush era encouraged banks such as Westpac (1817, originally Bank of New South Wales) and Commonwealth Bank of Australia (1911) to expand nationwide.

India, under British colonial rule, developed branch banking to facilitate trade, with institutions like the State Bank of India (1806, as Bank of Calcutta) and Punjab National Bank (1894) leading the way. France's industrial expansion and state-backed financial system fostered extensive branch networks through banks like Crédit Lyonnais (1863) and Société Générale (1864), while Germany's banking consolidation and industrial finance needs saw Deutsche Bank (1870) and Commerzbank (1870) adopt extensive branch models from the late 1800s. Japan, modernising its financial system during the Meiji Restoration (1868–1912), used branch banking to support economic growth, with institutions such as Sumitomo Bank (1895) and Mitsubishi Bank (1919, later part of MUFG) establishing extensive domestic and international networks.

Since then, the branch banking model has become pervasive, entrenched globally as the universally accepted way that banking happens. The branch banking model provides economies of scale, scope and geographic reach, while putting up barriers to entry. The logic is straightforward: a network of branches allows banks to spread costs – buildings, staff, security, compliance – across a large customer base, lowering the average cost per transaction. It also enables economies of scope, where a single location can offer everything from mortgages to wealth management, increasing revenue per customer.

This is why institutions like the previously mentioned Bank of Montreal, Lloyds Bank and the State Bank of India flourished early on, expanding their branch networks to establish themselves as dominant players in a market where trust in financial institutions depended on physical presence.

But context matters. The source of competitive edge in one world might be a yoke around your neck in another. Infrastructure comes with burdens. The cost of building and maintaining branches is enormous. This means outlying areas and small communities are left out and financial hubs – London, New York, Mumbai, São Paulo, Sydney, name your city of choice – are saturated with branches.

If banks were to operate as utilities, their mandate would shift from serving profitable customers to serving everyone – a model aimed at maximising social and economic inclusion rather than just profitability. Hernando de Soto and C.K. Prahalad's arguments underscore why broadening access is not just a moral imperative, but an economic one.[1] The challenge in achieving this in the model that has characterised the banking industry historically is not a matter of willingness but of simple economics: banks are run as a business, not a public utility. The Australian banking sector, dominated by a handful of major players like the Commonwealth Bank of Australia and Westpac, illustrates this. Despite the country's vast geography, branch expansion has always been selective, with the industry preferring profitable urban centres over remote areas, historically leaving many Australians reliant on post office banking services. The model's cost structure also means that the burden of financing branch networks is ultimately borne by customers. Higher service fees, lower interest on deposits and wider spreads on loans subsidise the upkeep of high-street locations and wooden-countered lobbies.

A tendency towards oligopoly is hardly rare in this sector. In the US, where regulators long resisted nationwide branch banking, the 1994 Riegle-Neal Interstate Banking and Branching Efficiency Act finally allowed banks to expand across state lines. This led to a wave of consolidation, with large institutions such as the Bank of America and Wells Fargo absorbing smaller regional banks. The result was a paradox: customers gained access to a larger network, but competition shrank as the industry coalesced around a few dominant players. This set of industry conditions has seen the number of Federal Deposit Insurance Corporation-insured commercial banks across the US decline from 14,483 in 1984 to 4,027 at the end of 2023, representing a 72.2% decrease.

These traits sum to a paradox in the traditional banking model. It confers a sense of permanence, security and legitimacy, but its cost structure ensures that it will never be truly inclusive. Banking, as it existed for 150 years, had a steady state of serving lots of people but not everyone. And increasingly, banks are in the business of managing costs by closing branches. In 1984, there were 41,311 branches across the US, rising to a peak of 81,809 branches in 2008. Although the annual change plateaued for a couple of years after the global financial crisis, it has been trending downwards since 2012, with an average of 808 bank branches closing each year over the past decade, so that at the end of 2023 there were 69,684 bank branches.[2]

Banks also face pressure to slash trading hours to manage the cost of servicing their branch networks. This is taken to near comedic excess in Malta. On the island with a population of just half a million people, high street branches open at 8.30am and close at 1.30pm on weekdays, and 12.30pm on Saturdays. Branches are closed all day Sunday.

The best of both worlds: Banking without limits

Enter the digital banking model – an idea foreseen as early as 1964 by the visionary Arthur C. Clarke Decades before the internet, Clarke anticipated a world where communication technology would dissolve the constraints of physical presence, enabling business, commerce and even essential services to function seamlessly across vast distances. His prediction was not just about convenience; it was about a fundamental restructuring of how societies operate. Banking, long tied to brick-and-mortar branches, would eventually be liberated from geography, allowing transactions, investments and financial services to exist beyond the confines of physical infrastructure. Clarke captured this transformation in a remarkable passage – and it is worth quoting him at length:

> But what about the city of the day after tomorrow – say the year 2000? I think it will be completely different; in fact, it may not even exist at all. Oh, I'm not thinking of the atom bomb and the next Stone Age. I'm thinking of the incredible breakthrough which has been made possible by developments in communications, particularly the transistor and, above all, the communication satellite. These things will make possible a world in which we can be in instant contact with each other wherever we may be – where we can contact our friends anywhere on Earth, even if we don't know their actual physical location. It will be possible in that age, perhaps only fifty years from now ... to conduct ... business from Tahiti or Bali just as well as ... from London. In fact, if it proves worthwhile, almost any executive skill, any administrative skill, even any physical skill, could be made independent of distance. I am perfectly serious when I suggest that one day we may have brain

surgeons in Edinburgh operating on patients in New Zealand. When that time comes, the whole world will have shrunk to a point.[3]

Clarke's vision was prescient. If a surgeon can operate remotely, you can pay suppliers with your phone. The digital banking revolution, long in the making, was not just about innovation but about a radical rethinking of what a financial institution could be in an era where presence was no longer a prerequisite for service – and might even be a poisoned chalice.

This is not to suggest that digital advances are better in every way. There are real drawbacks and barriers in making digital work. Most importantly, in their absolute form, digital services, by definition, do not have a human touch. The warmth of a conversation, the reassurance of a handshake, the trust built through face-to-face interactions are stripped away in the pursuit of efficiency and scale. Yet we are far more likely to trust an institution we can walk into, staffed by people we can see. But nobody said this had to be binary.

Between these two worlds lies the phygital model – a fusion of the high-touch, physical presence of traditional branch banking and the boundless, impersonal efficiency of digital banking. The challenge is to blend these elements seamlessly. The question is, how?

John Kane's Tyme Machine

This is the genius of Tyme's kiosk model. By embedding compact, technology-enabled kiosks in high-footfall retail locations, Tyme sidesteps the costs of full-scale branch banking, while retaining a physical touch-point for customer interaction. It allows for real human engagement where needed – onboarding, troubleshooting, building trust – while still leveraging the efficiencies of a digital-first bank. It is a hybrid banking model for the modern age, proving that in an industry caught between the weight of legacy and the relentless pull of technology, the answer is to do both, in just the right amount.

As Soichiro Honda is reported to have put it: 'Strategy is not always about choosing between "or" – sometimes, the real power lies in "and".'[4] Often innovation comes from combining seemingly opposing ideas – precision and speed, craftsmanship and mass production, tradition and disruption – rather than picking one.

TymeBank installed self-service kiosks inside popular retail locations such as Pick n Pay, Boxer and The Foschini Group (TFG) stores across South Africa, and later Robinsons retail stores in the Philippines. These kiosks allow customers to open a fully functional bank account in less than five minutes, using only their ID number and biometric verification. Within the same session, they receive a personalised Visa debit card, printed on-site – an immediate and tangible banking experience that removes the waiting period associated with some digital-first competitors.

Kiosks don't have to be self-service. Tyme injects the human touch strategically, making trained staff available on-site to help the less tech-savvy along.

TymeBank's kiosk strategy is particularly well suited to emerging markets, where financial exclusion remains a pervasive challenge. In countries with large unbanked populations, traditional banking expansion is slow and expensive, while digital-only solutions face adoption hurdles. Tyme threads a needle by placing kiosks in locations that customers already frequent, turning everyday retail spaces into financial access points.

Not without its challenges and challengers

This synergetic approach is not without detractors. Sometime in the early 2020s, Coen Jonker had a chat with Brett King, a fintech entrepreneur and banking futurist. King had a provocative question. Why, he wondered, did TymeBank bother with kiosks? All over the world, banks were shuttering branches and throwing money at people like King to help them digitise. Banks and fintechs were popping up with exclusively digital models. So, what was TymeBank – a supposedly innovative upstart – doing with a network of staffed kiosks in shopping malls? Wasn't that a little ... retro?

It wasn't the first time Jonker had heard that line of thinking. In fact, there were some in the Tyme team who felt King had a point.

By now, TymeBank had a substantial network of staffed electronic kiosks embedded in major retailers across South Africa. The model had propelled the bank's growth, bringing the founders closer to their dream of affordable, accessible banking for all South Africans. The kiosks were more than functional. They had become a part of the bank's DNA, a defining feature. But should they reconsider?

Kiosks had worked so far – the team could all agree on that. But they had to look to the future. If kiosks were destined to join the rotary phone, fax machines, slide projectors, floppy disks, CDs and traveller's cheques in the graveyard of outdated innovations, TymeBank would need to be ready.

They already had the playbook. In the Philippines, GoTyme had onboarded millions of customers without the same kiosk penetration as South Africa. But was South Africa ready to go fully digital? Or was the market uniquely unprepared to let go of physical touchpoints in banking?

The sexiest sound in banking

The Tyme team went back to the origin of the kiosk idea. Like the Wright brothers hunched over a splintered workbench, building a plane from cloth, spruce and second-hand bicycle gears, the Tyme team didn't start with elegance. They started with whatever they could get their hands on. No venture capital. No margin for error. Just a vision and a willingness to iterate until the damn thing flew.

The way Jonker describes the bootstrapping of the kiosks has shades of an episode of the 'Cautionary Tales' podcast by Tim Harford. He describes how Madame Clicquot, the 19th-century Champagne pioneer, devised a riddling rack in 1816 that allowed bottles to be rotated and tilted so that sediment could settle in the neck. This significantly enhanced Champagne production by improving the product's clarity and quality. This innovation gave Veuve Clicquot a competitive advantage, which allowed the firm to dominate the market. It took decades before competitors, including Jean-Rémy Moët, uncovered and adopted this technique. What Clicquot did with riddling racks, Tyme has perhaps done with kiosks – turning a messy prototype into an efficient manufacturing process. The tools were crude: Dieter Botha calls an early version a 'bucket with holes in it'. But the outcome is elegant: a robust, replicable interface that delivers just what is needed and nothing more.

Importantly, elegant doesn't mean elaborate. It means stripping away the unnecessary to reveal something that works beautifully. A parallel can be found in the evolution of digital music. At the turn of the century, MP3 players flooded the market. Many, like the Creative Nomad, were technical marvels, but hopelessly over-engineered. Buttons everywhere. Menus nested within menus. Models like the Nomad Jukebox Zen Xtra offered granular control but at the cost of usability. Users spent more time navigating than listening.

Then Apple released the iPod. It was revolutionary, not because it did more, but because it did less – with precision. A click wheel, a minimalist design and seamless integration with iTunes turned music into a frictionless experience. The iPod succeeded because Apple understood that true innovation removes obstacles.

Tyme's kiosks are the iPod of bank branches. What began as a messy prototype evolved into a system so intuitive that 80% of customers in South African and 55% in the Philippines now use it to onboard. In an industry known for bureaucracy and complexity, the kiosks simplify everything. No queues. No paperwork. No confusion. The lesson is clear: complexity is not a sign of sophistication. Simplicity – done well – is. And in that sense, Tyme's real innovation is not just technological. It is philosophical.

Like TymeBank itself, the kiosk model had not emerged perfectly formed. It was a vision that had staggered through faulty iterations, propped up at times by misplaced optimism and far-flung case studies. The model had three main components.

The first was the machine itself, or what John Kane called the Tyme Machine. 'I know it's terrible. So cheesy. I apologise,' he said on mentioning it in an interview. The first iteration, launched in 2012, was good at onboarding customers but 'about as reliable as a chocolate hammer in the Sahara'. The latest generation Tyme Machine is much more sophisticated. These self-service machines tackle one of the biggest headaches in South African banking: opening an account.

With TymeBank's kiosks, customers could open an account in less than five minutes. The kiosks also allowed TymeBank to comply with South Africa's Know Your Customer (KYC) regulations with far less friction. By using biometric verification (fingerprints) and integrating with the Department of Home Affairs, TymeBank could confirm new customer identities quickly and in full compliance with regulations. The part that really impressed customers was the moment when the machine spat out a personalised bank card with a little click. TymeBank's chief commercial officer, Cheslyn Jacobs, calls this 'the sexiest sound in banking'.

A conversation with almost any onboarded customer verifies this quickly. At a Totalsports store in Canal Walk, just outside Cape Town, a new TymeBank customer shared her experience: 'The kiosk was easy to find, the process was efficient, and it was amazing how each step was able to figure out who I was as part of verifying my identity. The ambassador was there to help, but the process was so easy that I was able to open the account without needing his help. And that I had my new bank card in my hand in five minutes was magic.' And so, back to Arthur C. Clarke: 'Any sufficiently advanced technology is indistinguishable from magic.'[5]

The second of three keystones of the kiosk model was the retail location. TymeBank needed a way to get to their customers. They had taken note of a successful banking model used in Brazil, where shopkeepers deep in the rainforest became agents of the bank.

So kiosks went to the customers. Just as important, they went to them in places they felt comfortable. Grocery stores like Pick n Pay and Boxer are widespread in South Africa. They are reliable and cost-effective. Some of that brand trust would surely rub off on TymeBank if they partnered with such strong brands.

Last, but not least, there are the kiosk ambassadors. Kane confirms that others, including PEP Stores, had attempted the Brazilian approach of doubling shopkeepers up as bank agents. The South African experiment said this idea was dead on arrival.

Retail staff, it turned out, made lousy bank ambassadors. Turnover was high and motivation was low. 'It worked well in Brazil because that person, that local shop, was the centre of a local community,' says Kane.

This is where the third component comes into the picture. TymeBank introduced ambassadors, human assistants from the local community who were on hand to help anyone who struggled with the self-service machines. These envoys could lead customers through the digital processes, answer questions and build trust, especially among those new to banking or uneasy with purely digital interactions. They were arguably the secret sauce of the whole operation. Our Canal Walk customer's experience reinforces this: 'He was friendly, and ready to help, although the process was so simple that I was able to open the account while he stayed in the background just in case.' This three-part model is clever, quick, efficient, seamless, engaging tech-with-touch, and, crucially, it is cheap.

Low cost, not 'no cost'

The kiosk model offered staggering cost savings. TymeBank's figures show that a kiosk can be set up for 1/500th of the cost of a physical bank branch. Game changer! 'We could onboard a customer for US$4,' says Kane, 'which is revolutionary.' Most of those savings could be passed on to the consumer, allowing TymeBank to offer its customers the lowest transaction charges in the industry, zero fixed fees and higher interest rates on savings accounts compared to competitors.

Nevertheless, the low-cost kiosk model was not 'no cost'. The kiosks, though tough and sturdy, required regular maintenance and updating. Every component was essential. 'The fingerprint scanner could fail. The tablet screen could fail, the printer could fail, the PC board could fail,' explains Jacobs. And any downtime wasn't just inconvenient – it was a reputational risk. It would be like visiting your bank branch and finding it closed. As the kiosk network grew, so did the maintenance costs and the operational headaches. The bank was already on version six of its kiosk, and TymeBank faced an almost complete fleet replacement at the end of 2024, which required rolling out 500 kiosks in the space of six months. This was no mean feat, Jacobs acknowledges.

The team had something of Edison about them. The optimism wasn't cosmetic – it was industrial grade. Edison tested a thousand filaments before one worked. The team burnt through models, markets and near misses with the same ferocity. It was exhausting. But it worked.

There was no question that the kiosk model was cheaper than a nationwide branch network, but branches were never on the table. Compared to a purely digital model – no machines, no staff, no maintenance – the costs were still impressive. Two numbers evidence this. First, customer acquisition cost: TymeBank's customer acquisition cost ranks among the lowest in the world. Second, with operating expenditure per customer of US$17 per annum, this is somewhere between a third and a tenth of the figure for South Africa's Big-Five retail banks.

The gains and pains of partnership

TymeBank's take on the Brazilian rainforest model involved partnerships with some of South Africa's retail heavyweights. More than 28 million South Africans walk into a Pick n Pay or Boxer store every year; and TFG is the country's largest retail clothing group, with 30 leading brands and over 2,800 outlets.[6]

But not all partnerships work. Tyme experienced this with MTN. And learnt the lessons. 'Partnerships can only sustain if it strengthens the core of each other,' says Van der Walt. 'It has to make financial sense for both partners and requires a basic premise of trust as the default – this is where energy comes from.'

'Our partnerships with the likes of Pick n Pay, Boxer and TFG have been vital to our business model,' says Jacobs. 'They provide us with the physical presence we need to reach our customers without the overhead of maintaining our own branch network. It's a win-win situation; we get the space and the customer access, and they get the benefit of offering a banking service that adds value to their customers' shopping experience.'

TFG deepened the partnership by covering 50% of manufacturing and maintenance costs for the kiosks, along with debit card and KYC expenses. In exchange for a piece of the long-term profits, they also chipped in a

30% subsidy for in-field ambassador costs, which accounts for about 61% of TymeBank's customer acquisition cost. The Pick n Pay and Boxer partnerships came with another strategic perk: exclusive access to one of South Africa's most popular loyalty programmes, Smart Shopper, with over 9 million members. This was a major advantage to the bank in reaching its target market.

TymeBank's positioning play was informed by well-documented corporate strategy. The 'prime location strategy' had already proven its worth in other spheres. The oft-cited example in boardrooms is fast-fashion retailer Zara. The brand relies on footfall rather than traditional advertising to drive visibility and sales. Its stores are strategically placed in high-traffic areas – especially in key fashion hubs like Paris, New York and London – where regularly updated window displays serve as live advertising. The strategy is so effective that Zara spends just 0.3% of its revenue on advertising, far below the industry average of 3.5%. By focusing on store location, Zara turns high footfall into a key driver of brand awareness and customer engagement.[7]

TymeBank's kiosks worked on the same principle. They made the brand not just visible but tangible. 'In a market where people still question digital-only banks, a physical touchpoint is a key differentiator,' says Jacobs. 'We know how powerful that physical artefact is.' That lesson was learnt in the early days of TymeBank when the bank allowed customers to open a cardless bank account. 'And when we launched that offering,' says Jacobs, 'there was basically no adoption. The fact that there was no physical piece of plastic meant that no customers believed what they actually had was a bank account.' TymeBank's ambassadors could simply have helped customers open an account on their smartphones, but there was something about the physical presence of the machines that made the bank real. Like the fabricated shutter noise on a digital camera, the kiosks made banking with TymeBank feel more familiar, more like traditional banking. And that is what South African customers wanted.

Placing kiosks in stores also came with a degree of operational risk. Like a creature reliant on its habitat, TymeBank's kiosks were at the mercy of their retail roommates. Should a partner decide to shrink its footprint, remodel its store or shift its strategic focus, the network could take a hit. Reports of financial strain on Pick n Pay are a case in point. Roughly half (500) of the kiosk network was in Pick n Pay stores. So, when Pick n Pay, after a run of business challenges, announced in May 2024 that it would shut one in ten corporate supermarkets (those not owned by franchisees), as part of a restructuring plan, the vulnerability of the kiosk model came into focus.[8]

'We see it's a risky business,' Jacobs says. 'We're not the ones selling directly here. Our dependence on retailers is always going to run the risk of leaving us open to any alteration in the ways those companies do business. How can we find ways to reduce some of that risk and yet continue to service our customers at a level that's acceptable to them?' That was a question the team would need to consider, Jacobs adds.

Despite its difficulties, partnering is in Tyme's blood. Van der Walt certainly brings a reputation for partnership building. His spell with the Foundation for Research Development involved bringing together government, industry and academia to build centres of excellence. We see this in the group's various partnerships with a multitude of types of partners.

Context is key

TymeBank has enjoyed great success in South Africa. And, learning from this model, GoTyme has enjoyed tremendous success in the Philippines – albeit with far fewer kiosks per capita. This is a healthy reminder that what works in Manzini doesn't necessarily work in Manila – or, at least, not in the same way.

Madame Clicquot is instructive here, too. She didn't just transform Champagne production with her riddling table. She was a pioneer of international expansion. During the Napoleonic Wars, she secretly shipped 10,000 bottles of her 1811 vintage to Russia, winning over the local nobility. She understood their love for ultra-sweet Champagne – much sweeter than what was popular in France – so she adjusted her product to match their taste perfectly.

She didn't stop at selling to the elite. By making Champagne feel both luxurious and within reach, she opened the door to a whole new market. As Tim Harford points out, she turned Champagne into the go-to drink for celebrations, not just for the rich but for everyone. By the time she passed away in 1866, her brand had gone global, with sales skyrocketing from 17,000 bottles in 1811 to 750,000.

Madame Clicquot's expansion was the 19th-century version of what today's tech giants like Apple or Google do – scaling up fast and dominating the market. Sure, it took her 50 years instead of the five or ten we expect from modern startups, but the formula for success hasn't changed: find the right market, time your move and grow smartly through top-notch execution.

Both the Philippines and South Africa are youthful nations. In the Philippines, over half of the population is under the age of 25, while, in South Africa, that figure is similarly high at 44%. Young populations tend to be more adaptable to change, especially when it comes to adopting new technologies. In both countries, digital banking is on the rise, but the Philippines has shown a particularly strong inclination towards fully digital onboarding. A 2021 FICO survey found that 56% of Filipino consumers prefer digital channels for engaging with their banks, and the Bangko Sentral ng Pilipinas (BSP) reports that 65% of adults used digital payments in 2021, up sharply from 43% in 2019.[9] Beyond these internal market drivers, Van der Walt also suspects that adoption in the Philippines has a lot to do with 'how Tyme has positioned the brand more towards a mass affluent market compared to where Tyme started in South Africa'. In typical Tyme fashion, he closes off his comment with, 'But let's see what the data tells us.'

Notwithstanding the drivers, the momentum in the Philippines is supported by growing digital infrastructure, government-backed fintech innovation and strong mobile penetration. Filipino consumers, especially younger users, are increasingly comfortable managing their financial lives through smartphones and apps, making them well prepared for digital-first banking. South Africa is on a similar path, but with different starting points. While mobile banking is rapidly growing, gaps in digital infrastructure and financial inclusion still create friction for some customers. That said, the same underlying opportunity exists: a young, connected population ready to embrace better, faster and more affordable ways to bank.

The experience in South Africa with kiosk usage also helps add colour to the story of the phygital model. The kiosk on its own isn't enough. In the beginning, TymeBank had around 600 kiosks, but just 400 were manned by ambassadors. 'The [other] 200 kiosks literally became ornaments,' said Jacobs. 'We were stubborn. We created this kiosk, it is super intuitive, very self-service. Customers must press a couple of buttons on the screen and within five minutes the process is done ... But people just don't do it because it's so far removed from what is accepted as normal in banking.'

The difference was stark: manned kiosks were six to eight times more productive than the unmanned kiosks. This reflects the country's vast digital divide. Many South Africans, particularly in the communities TymeBank serves, are still catching up on digital literacy and access. Data across the sector shows that while mobile phone ownership is high (over 89%), the share of people actively using mobile banking apps remains low (43%), and reliable internet access and trust remain uneven.[10]

TymeBank's extensive roll-out of over 1,000 kiosks plays to that context. In South Africa, all TymeBank's kiosks are staffed and 80% of their customers are now onboarded through that channel.

'What we see, particularly in emerging markets, is that there is still a place for human engagement in building trust, even in digital markets,' says Jacobs. To build the credibility needed to turn new users into loyal customers, TymeBank recruited hyper-locally. This meant that staff understood the local community and could speak to customers in their first language. It was a smart strategy that lowered cultural and social barriers between the customers and the brand – no small feat in a country as diverse and fragmented as South Africa.

Kiosk ambassadors also had to pass a litmus test in their job interviews.

If they had not opened their own TymeBank account, the interview was ended. The thinking was that if they didn't believe in the product, they couldn't sell it. That personal buy-in translated into a more authentic brand promotion and stronger customer trust.

In 2024, TymeBank achieved a net promoter score of 61%, reflecting the highest level of customer satisfaction in its peer group.[11] And TymeBank now ranks sixth among 37 banks in the Consumer Trust Index – an overall assessment of how much the brand and the company behind it are trusted.

The copycat problem
The kiosk model was innovative. It set TymeBank apart from competitors. But the model was not impossible to replicate. There was nothing to stop the big banks – or even a new digital bank – from introducing their own kiosks. If that happened, the bank would lose its competitive edge. It would need to consider how to differentiate further, possibly by integrating more advanced digital solutions that could complement or replace the physical kiosks.[12]

Jacobs has shrugged off the risk of imitation kiosks. 'I don't think there's a big bank in this country that is prepared to cannibalise what they have already built,' he says. 'I think there has been one or two that have tried. I think I can say they failed. The reality of our model is high volume, low margin. For them to even think about doing what we've done, they would have to eat their own lunch first. They've just got way too much to lose. And I also think they'll get massive backlash if they have to start closing branches.' If anything, he says, copycats are validation that TymeBank is doing things right. And if anyone tries to beat them at their own game, Jacobs is confident Tyme's first-mover advantage would keep them on top. Van der Walt also suspects that 'there will be a need for branches in the market for a long time to come still, but Tyme will take a disproportionate share of the market as people start to trust digital banking more'.

The future is phygital
'TymeBank has truly made remarkable progress in little time,' remarks

Brett King. But, as a challenger, he urged that the bank had to think ahead and consider 'whether what we are investing in kiosks is money that could be better spent on improving our digital capabilities'. This is a debate for another day. As it stands, digital-first, with the kicker of kiosks with the ambassadors, is the winning formula. For now, South Africans are not clamouring for pure digitisation. In fact, the top two queries on TymeBank's social media feeds are: 'When will Tyme get their own branches?' and 'When will Tyme get their own ATMs?'

The kiosks fulfil a subtly different purpose in the Philippines. In that context, they use an elegant and aspirational Tiffany Blue product colour to fuse with their 'beautiful experience' tagline. Social media has been a powerful promoter, with sites showing customers expressing delight in their beautiful, freshly minted kiosk cards. @jhasminesmyll is one of thousands of TikTok members that describes the card as 'beautiful', alongside the benefits of ownership, including 5% interest per annum on deposits, three times reward points when the card is used at a Robertsons store, no minimum balance and three free transfers to other banks each week.[13]

And then there is the celebrated GoTyme walking man. In a striking celebration of reaching 5 million users, GoTyme Bank orchestrated an innovative spectacle involving 'The Victor', a prominent 55-metre-tall statue located near their headquarters in Bridgetowne, Quezon City. This monumental figure became the centrepiece of a dynamic marketing campaign that seamlessly blended art, technology and brand storytelling.[14]

The kiosks also represent a way for Tyme to outcompete local banks. 'Bank services in the Philippines are appalling,' says Lionel (Lion) Gacad, chief experience officer at GoTyme. 'It can take a bank 30 to 45 minutes to respond to a call. Then you press 1 through 9, and again 1 through 9 – and then you might get cut off.'

Lion's aim is to build a business that customers love, not like, and to build this at scale with 'human in the loop' using AI. Using the phone as a personal banker is the first step. 'Tech stacks in the Philippines are so old,' he goes on, 'that if you make a withdrawal from an ATM and cash doesn't come out, it can take seven to ten days for a refund. What if you need the cash now?

'Tyme will refund the customer in less than 30 minutes. We do this by putting cash at risk to achieve customer appeasement. The risk is always that the cash does not come back, but that is the case in only 1% of transactions. This is a cost, but it builds very high messaging to the customer. Other banks use customer deflection and chat bots to shield bank people from customers. This turns the customer experience into a dismal journey.'

Contrary to initial speculations of digital manipulation, the statue's movement was a meticulously planned event by GoTyme Bank. 'The Victor' was animated to step away from its original position, traversing towards Robinsons Giga Tower – GoTyme Bank's head office – where it symbolically installed the bank's logo. This act not only marked the bank's significant milestone but also underscored its commitment to innovation and forward momentum.[15]

The choice of 'The Victor' as a symbol is deeply resonant; its depiction of a figure in mid-stride with a raised fist embodies themes of victory, advancement and relentless pursuit of goals – qualities that align seamlessly with GoTyme Bank's ethos. By animating the statue, the bank conveyed a message of breaking boundaries and moving beyond traditional constraints, much like their approach to modern banking.

This captivating event served as more than just a celebration; it was a strategic initiative to drive engagement and direct attention to GoTyme's innovative phygital banking model. By capturing public interest through the moving statue, the bank effectively highlighted its blend of digital convenience and physical accessibility. The spectacle encouraged both existing and potential customers to explore GoTyme's services, particularly drawing attention to their in-store kiosks, where individuals can seamlessly open accounts and receive personalised assistance.

The campaign exemplifies how experiential marketing can be harnessed to create buzz, reinforce brand identity and drive customer interaction. By intertwining cultural landmarks with corporate milestones, GoTyme Bank not only celebrated its achievement but also strengthened its connection with the community, inviting them to be part of their ongoing journey towards innovative banking solutions.

That would have likely fallen flat in South Africa. It is another example of a tightrope that Tyme must walk. Scale demands a generic backend that can perform all the functions of a modern bank. However, on the ground, Tyme – whatever shape it takes – must be adaptive, responsive and, despite the backend, a local brand for local consumers.

Chapter 11

Going Beyond Borders

The decision to reject one paradigm is always simultaneously the decision to accept another, and the judgment leading to that decision involves the comparison of both paradigms with nature and with each other.

— Thomas Kuhn

'All models are wrong. Some are useful.' The truism is as relevant today as it was in 1976 when British statistician George Box coined the phrase. Models aren't meant to be slavishly followed. They are best wielded as guides to direct our thinking. Where reality demands it, we should depart from the model. That doesn't make the model bad. In fact, the model can typically take credit for pointing us to the smart way of breaking it.

Entrepreneurs are especially adept at breaking models. They make bold but calculated moves that often seem to fly in the face of established best practice – and that separates luck and chance from design and skill. Of course, that means that entrepreneurial endeavours fail at high rates. That is part of the deal, and the figures speak to this. According to the *Global Startup Ecosystem Report*, approximately 11 out of 12 startups (about 92%) eventually fail.[1] But when founders make considered departures that smash a model with purpose, they have a shot at changing the world.

And the world is the goal. That comes naturally to entrepreneurs. In case it needs evidence, a recent McKinsey report shows that for the world's largest 3,000 listed companies, half of all growth in the decade up to 2019 came from foreign markets.[2] Once you have a foothold at home, real growth is over borders. This push is elevated when your home market faces structural growth stagnation or when your model demands scale that is only available beyond your home market.

The question is, which borders do you cross? In an early conversation with Coen Jonker, we asked what seemed like an obvious question: why did Tyme choose to expand first into Southeast Asia, rather than follow a more conventional path of international growth? After all, traditional models might suggest starting with closer markets in sub-Saharan Africa, where large, fast-growing and underserved markets could offer a local competitive advantage. Or, if the strategy was to aim further afield, why not target India? With 1.45 billion people and an economy that has grown at an impressive 6.4% annually over the past 20 years – double the global average – India might appear a more compelling opportunity than the combined sub-Saharan market, which has 1.1 billion people and an average growth rate of 3.9% per annum.

Jonker's response is a clear example of second-order thinking – that all-too-rare ability to consider immediate outcomes and follow a chain of causation back to its origins and forward to later effects and the reactions that will come along the way.[3]

The rules of expansion

In these discussions with Jonker, he explained that Tyme would not be pursuing India any time soon. The market was exactly as we described, but with the additional attribute of being highly competitive. Everyone was there because they saw the exact same thing as each other.[4] This translates into low profit margins, high innovation pressure, the risk of rapid market shifts, and intense branding and marketing demands.[5] This is hardly the stuff of competitive strategy. And while various African markets were geographically close, in similar times zones and in many instances culturally proximate, Tyme had instead chosen to go to the Philippines. With hindsight, this seemed like a stroke of genius.

But why on earth was Tyme there at all? Hindsight may be an exact science, but surely, we challenged Jonker, foresight would not have singled out the Philippines as an obvious choice. After all, the Philippines is a sprawling archipelago of over 7,000 islands, presenting significant logistical and operational challenges. The country's complex history, shaped by Spanish colonial rule and a unique blend of Asian and Western influences, creates a distinct cultural and regulatory landscape – and there are over 170 languages spoken across the archipelago. Then, a time difference of six hours from South Africa makes coordinating operations, managing teams and maintaining effective communication a further challenge.

Moreover, the Philippines has often struggled with perceptions of bureaucracy and red tape. They rank moderately on the World Bank's Ease of Doing Business Index. The country has also faced well-documented issues with crime, including the controversial war on drugs under President Rodrigo Duterte, which cast a shadow over the stability and predictability of the business environment.

The Philippines faces the same challenges dogging digital banks across the region. Chief among them is the struggle to grow quickly without burning through cash. Lacking the built-in audiences of super apps or e-commerce giants, many digital banks are forced to spend heavily on marketing and incentives to attract customers, a strategy that rarely delivers sustainable economics. Even when they succeed in attracting deposits with high interest rates, the next step proves elusive: turning those deposits into profitable loans or fee-generating services. As a result, many banks end up with costly liabilities and little revenue to show for it.

Lending to the unbanked, an often-touted advantage of digital banks, has proven riskier than many expected. Thin credit files and unreliable data make assessing risk difficult, resulting in deteriorating asset quality and forcing some banks to retreat to the safer, established customer base already dominated by traditional banks. Regulation, meanwhile, remains uneven. Although improving, the support enjoyed by early movers in other markets is largely absent here, leaving newcomers to navigate a fog of uncertainty.

To make matters even more challenging for a new entrant, conventional banks have not been idle. Many have invested heavily in technology, closing the digital gap and, in some cases, outperforming their nimbler rivals. Digital banks now find themselves squeezed from both sides, struggling to build profitable business models, while incumbents sharpen their digital offerings. Building a slick app is one thing; building a profitable, differentiated and sustainable business is quite another.

If digital banks cannot achieve real differentiation and achieve profitability quickly, they risk getting swallowed up by the same big, established players they were trying to challenge. We have already seen this play out to an extent across Asia.

Despite these obstacles, Tyme saw an opportunity that others might have missed – an insight that would only become clear with the benefit of second-order thinking.

At first glance, it makes no sense. A business formed in South Africa and just approaching profitability at home doesn't race across the planet to the Philippines. There is too much to overcome: the Philippine peso is prone to fluctuations against major currencies, and the country's vulnerability to natural disasters, from typhoons to earthquakes, brings operational and insurance challenges that would add a layer of risk to the new market entrant. The infrastructure gap is another hurdle.

While Metro Manila and a few key cities boast modern amenities, much of the country remains underdeveloped, with inconsistent access to reliable utilities and transportation networks. There is also a structural challenge in the financial sector itself. The Philippines has a highly concentrated banking market, dominated by a few established local players with deep-rooted relationships and a prickly demeanour towards competition.

Add to this a complex regulatory environment, where navigating permits, approvals and compliance can be labyrinthine, often requiring strong local partnerships and an understanding of the nuances of both national and provincial governance. There is also the political undercurrent – the Philippines' democracy is vibrant but sometimes unpredictable, with policy shifts that can catch even seasoned investors off guard.

Given these layers of complexity, Tyme's choice to enter the Philippines wasn't just adventurous – it appeared, at first glance, to defy rational business strategy. But, as Jonker would explain, there was a method to the madness – a strategic rationale that would quickly be revealed.

Conventional thinking, supported by decades of evidence, suggests that the most sensible approach to internationalisation is to 'go close and go small'. This usually means pursuing a regional strategy rather than a global one. For Tyme, that would imply testing smaller, nearby markets like Botswana or Namibia, where cultural and regulatory familiarity provide a gentler learning curve.[6]

Bolder movers might look further afield to Nigeria, with its vast population of 237 million, or Egypt, home to 118 million people. The Democratic Republic of Congo, with 113 million citizens, also presents a tempting prize. Others might prefer the familiarity of developed markets like Australia or the US, where regulatory frameworks, consumer behaviour and business practices feel more predictable.

None of this implies that these seemingly obvious expansion routes are straightforward. Far from it. The South African corporate graveyard is littered with ambitious ventures that faltered abroad. Shoprite's exit from Nigeria after 15 years of struggle highlighted the difficulties of navigating complex regulatory environments and supply chain challenges. Woolworths' costly failure in Australia, which resulted in a US$1 billion write-down, demonstrated how cultural misalignment and poor strategic fit can unravel even the most carefully planned expansion.

PPC's venture into the Democratic Republic of Congo faced political instability, low demand and fierce competition, proving how even the most calculated expansions can go wrong. Telkom's attempt to enter Nigeria ended in a bruising withdrawal after years of battling poor infrastructure and inadequate returns.

The lesson from these failures is clear: regional proximity or cultural familiarity offers no guarantees of success. It takes more than geographic convenience or demographic potential to thrive in new markets. For Tyme, the challenge was to avoid becoming another name on the long list of South African corporates that misread the complexities of international expansion.

The Philippines is no one-horse town, either. With a population of 115 million, it is the 14th largest country in the world by this metric. Of course, although India and China offered scale in a single step, the markets were highly competitive. The corporate corpses on the 'Let's do China or India Hill' are many. On this, Jonker's logic fits with Silicon Valley icon Peter Thiel's famous line: 'Competition is for losers.' In Jonker's words, 'Everyone is there already!'

Team Tyme also wasn't naive about the Philippines. When we asked GoTyme's Nate Clarke over a dinner in Manila which South African companies had successfully made their way into the Philippines, his reply was: 'That's a tough one. There's only three that come to mind: Aspen Pharmacare, Cartrack and former South African mining giant Goldfields.' The Philippines is not an obvious destination for South African firms looking for new markets.

Tyme travel

Mainstream strategists might offer a reassuringly rational account of how companies can succeed when expanding across borders. The logic is straightforward: identify an attractive foreign market, leverage existing advantages and watch the profits roll in. Rinse and repeat to build an empire. Economic theory, after all, suggests that firms will thrive abroad if they possess a competitive edge – be it through cost efficiency, brand strength or proprietary know-how. And it can work. However, the go-to examples might lure us in with an availability bias. Nike may be everywhere, but it is not the norm.

Reality is a graveyard of failed international expansions: Walmart in Germany, Target in Canada, Home Depot and Uber in China, Tesco in the US, Starbucks in Australia and McDonald's in Bolivia. These high-profile examples prove the rule: bold international expansion strategies – even if underpinned by big brands and hefty balance sheets – can be quickly undone by misjudged market dynamics, cultural blind spots, operational inefficiencies and strategic missteps. And this suggests that the conventional wisdom is missing something fundamental. The question is: what? And the answer helps give colour to Tyme's strategy and success.

Too many business theories take a mechanistic view of global expansion, assuming that what works in one market should, with minor adjustments, work elsewhere. The comparative advantage model suggests that firms will naturally succeed in foreign markets where they can exploit lower production costs or superior technology. Tyme has both, but this is not specific to the Philippines, and it applies equally to most potential markets.

The institutional theory approach argues that companies will thrive in countries with familiar legal and regulatory structures. This would make Australia, Botswana, Canada, Malaysia and Namibia more obvious destinations for Tyme than the Philippines.

Meanwhile, the resource-based view holds that firms with strong brands, unique products or superior capabilities will translate these strengths seamlessly into new markets. See the list of fraught expansions above. How's that working out for you?

And, according to the ownership-location-internalisation model, multinational success is largely a function of having the right mix of proprietary assets, favourable host-market conditions and control over operations. Perhaps Tyme ticks this box at home, but this doesn't make setting up shop in Manila an obvious choice.

Breaking out of your CAGE

In scouring the evidence of successful international expansion, Pankaj Ghemawat, Professor of Management and Strategy at New York University's Stern School of Business, pulls a strategic rabbit from the hat of globalisation.

In his work, 'Distance Still Matters: The Hard Reality of Global Expansion', Ghemawat argues that companies often overestimate the ease of international expansion and underestimate the impact of distance. Here he includes geographical distance, but it also covers cultural, administrative and economic 'distance'.[7]

A wealth of literature and practical experience helps make sense of this complex reality, and the logic of the CAGE model is straightforward: the closer two countries are on the four metrics of culture (C), administration (A), geography (G) and economic distance (E), the more likely a business is to succeed when crossing the border between the two countries. From this framework, things that bring countries closer, according to the CAGE Distance Framework, include cultural factors like a shared language, similar social norms and common religious beliefs; administrative factors like historical ties, trade agreements and similar legal systems; geographic factors like shared borders, proximity and good transport links; and economic factors like similar income levels, trade relationships and labour costs.

Firms do not expand into a vacuum. They enter societies with cultures, entrenched political systems and unique ways of doing business. The ability to enter new geographies presents digital banks with the potential for exponential growth, but also exposes them to unfamiliar regulatory environments, cultural differences and operational risks.[8]

Ghemawat illustrates the CAGE model with an example. Star TV, launched in Hong Kong in 1991, was widely expected to be a slam dunk in Asia, banking on the assumption that the region's newly wealthy, 'media-starved' elite would embrace English-language satellite programming. Star sought to sidestep the cost of creating local content and instead deliver Western-style television to an affluent, advertising-friendly audience. Rupert Murdoch was so confident in this strategy that between 1993 and 1995, his company, News Corporation, acquired Star in tranches for a cumulative US$825 million. Then reality happened.

Asian audiences largely rejected English-language programming in favour of local-language content, and Star struggled against entrenched domestic broadcasters. By 1999, the company had accumulated losses equal to roughly the purchase price. What was envisioned as an effortless media expansion instead became a high-profile failure, illustrating the steep costs of underestimating cultural and administrative distance in global markets.

In hindsight, Murdoch's bad Star deal looks particularly naive. Sure, it is an archetypical tale of ignoring the C in CAGE. But it demonstrates Ghemawat's point beautifully.

Uber's struggles in China, Tesco's failed US expansion and Starbucks' missteps in Australia all stemmed from a common issue: misreading the local market. Uber could not outmanoeuvre strong, well-entrenched local competitors like DiDi, which had better regulatory connections and local insights. Tesco's Fresh & Easy venture in the US flopped because it misjudged American shopping habits, particularly the preference for larger supermarkets and established brands. Starbucks misread Australia's deeply ingrained café culture, where independent, high-quality coffee shops dominated. In each case, it was not just about dealing with tough competition – it was about getting the market dynamics wrong.

Too often, firms expand based on market size rather than market fit. Walmart assumed German consumers would embrace its low-cost, high-service model; instead, they baulked at greeters and resisted bulk shopping. eBay presumed that its auction-style platform would work in China, failing to grasp the importance of guanxi (the local relationship-based business culture), handing the market to Alibaba's Taobao. In each case, the companies' strategic playbooks overlooked the human, political and economic realities that shape commerce.

The real question for executives, then, goes beyond the obvious consideration of whether a foreign market is big. Big is fine. But is it navigable by us today and for the foreseeable future? That is much harder to decipher than 'is it big?'.

Ghemawat's framework reminds us that successful expansion requires not just scale but adaptation – an appreciation that business, at its core, is shaped by institutions, norms and structures that no spreadsheet can fully capture. Global ambition must be matched with local intelligence. Strategy, after all, is not just about opportunity – it's about overcoming distance.

Jonker wasn't blind to CAGE. As a South African who served as group executive for International Financial Services for one of the ten biggest banks in the world, his eyes were wide open to the many reasons it was risky to take a digital bank from South Africa to the Philippines. But he also knew the tremendous benefits waiting for the first bank to get this sort of move right. This wasn't the first time Jonker had needed to explain his thinking. We could tell. He had it down. And changed our sceptical minds.

Jonker had ways to strategically break out of this cage, acknowledging the locked gates and exploiting the sleeping sentries that most haven't noticed.

The CAGE Distance between South Africa and the Philippines is relatively high.

Culturally, the two nations diverge in language, ethnic composition and social norms, although they share strong religious influences, with Christianity playing a central role in both societies. Administratively, they lack historical colonial ties or common legal systems. While both are members of global organisations like the World Trade Organization and the United Nations, they have no significant bilateral trade agreements.

Geographically, the distance between them is vast, with a time-zone gap of six hours, although their access to seaports facilitates maritime trade.

Economically, while their income per capita ranges are somewhat comparable, South Africa's economy is largely resource-based, whereas the Philippines relies heavily on services and remittances. Both countries contend with sizeable informal sectors and are integrated into global trade, albeit through distinct industries – mining and manufacturing in South Africa and business process outsourcing in the Philippines.

These factors collectively create considerable distance, making deep economic integration between the two countries more challenging. Put simply, Ghemawat's CAGE framework suggests that Tyme would do well to be looking in places other than the Philippines.

But the important McKinsey work has a further word to offer. In its study of the world's 3,000 largest listed companies, Rebecca Doherty and her co-authors show that regardless of where a company is based, venturing abroad makes sense only if you first excel at home. They suggest that 'beating local' means having an exportable competitive advantage that also enables a firm to be a market leader, and that the firm needs to be able to win profitable market share from local competitors in their destination region.[9]

Without a transferable source of advantage, a company will simply be competing head-on with local players that are more established and have a better understanding of the local context. We would venture that Tyme evidences the 'beating local' duo by a wide margin, including gathering significant market share in the low-income segment at home, and cost of customer acquisition and cost of customer management that rank among the lowest in the world, coupled with market-leading net promoter scores in their 'home' market.

Time for a reality check. We put this to Neill Young and Sarah-Jane Alexander one day. As investment professionals at Coronation Fund Managers, they know these dynamics. Their response was sobering. 'Even if the cost of customer acquisition is among the lowest in the world, what ultimately matters is revenue per customer. Put that up against the cost of acquiring and managing the customer.' They struggle to imagine Tyme growing sufficient scale.

There is one last piece to the puzzle of successful expansion, and it helps square away the challenges raised in Ghemawat's CAGE framework. The McKinsey study shows that whether you are a business model pioneer, commodity player, product innovator or brand builder, the companies get the best foothold in their target market by acquiring – or partnering – with a local player. In the case of their expansion to the Philippines, Tyme did both.

In launching GoTyme in the Philippines in October 2022, Tyme forged a powerful joint venture with the Gokongwei Group – one of the country's largest and most diversified conglomerates. Through its holding company, JG Summit Holdings, the group balance sheet reflects total assets of US$18.9 billion and operates across multiple sectors, including food and beverage, air transportation, real estate, petrochemicals and financial services, generating net income of US$400 million per year off annual revenue of US$6.9 billion.

Tyme needed a local retail partner that could help it break through the barriers of distance, culture, administration and economics. That breakthrough came in a moment of unexpected chemistry. In a short online meeting, held under Covid-era restrictions and lasting less than an hour, Jonker and Lance Gokongwei immediately clicked. It was, in Jonker's words, 'a moment of magic'. What followed was a partnership that would open the door for Tyme's entry into the Philippines and

PART IV: THE SECOND TYME

become a textbook case of Tyme's strength in structuring high-trust, high-functioning partnerships.

Varun Mittal recalls how quickly the fit became clear: 'In the space of two weeks, Coen met with eight family groups. The Gokongwei family stood out by a long way – their retail footprint was strong, they understood the consumer's bias for physical presence and their reputation was stellar.' At that first online meeting, after hearing Jonker tell the Tyme story, Lance Gokongwei simply said, 'I think we need more than an hour,' and asked if Coen could stay on the call. One week later, the two sides had signed a memorandum of understanding.

Remarkably, Jonker and Gokongwei met in person for the first time more than two years later at the official launch of GoTyme in Manila.

In the first few moments of our meeting with Gokongwei, it was clear why he was enthused by the potential of Tyme within minutes of meeting Jonker. 'The Philippines had too many banks, but Filipinos are underbanked – and specifically digitally underbanked. And the Gokongwei Group offers Tyme a powerful competitive advantage through its retail footprint.'

That footprint is vast. Built by John Gokongwei Jr, the conglomerate spans supermarkets, department stores, hardware chains, pharmacies and convenience stores, all under Robinsons Retail Holdings, Inc. – a network of over 2,200 stores. Banking was already part of the group's empire through Robinsons Bank, a well-established institution with a traditional branch network, later merged into BPI. But GoTyme was something different. It wasn't just another bank – it was a leap forward.

Tyme's digital banking expertise, combined with the Gokongwei Group's retail presence, offered a model that circumvented the usual constraints of brick-and-mortar banking. Instead of expensive branches, GoTyme could use retail stores as onboarding hubs, bringing banking services to everyday Filipinos with the ease of a digital-first experience. For the Gokongwei Group, it was an opportunity to leapfrog past legacy banking models and position itself at the forefront of the Philippines' digital banking revolution.

Lance Gokongwei recognises a number of risks and threats to GoTyme, specifically, and the digital banking model, more generally. These include the issuing of new licences by the Bangko Sentral ng Pilipinas (BSP), with some of the biggest digital banks, including Revolut, rumoured to be interested; unanticipated regulatory changes; higher reserve requirements; competition as incumbents build digital solutions; or the inability to monetise clients.

While these risks are real – and the requirement is to manage them – the size of the opportunity that the Philippines affords Tyme is unmistakable. Through Robinsons, the partnership comes to life at street level. A visit to any Robinsons Supermarket, Robinsons Department Store, No Brand, Robinsons Easymart or Southstar Drug quickly shows why. GoTyme kiosks sit right at the entrance to the stores, staffed by assistants who can onboard a customer in minutes – replicating the South African model.

Customer behaviour does differ between the two societies. In South Africa, most registration is done entirely at a kiosk. In the Philippines, people are more likely to sign up using the app. The kiosk is then a convenient way to get your card printed.

The process is seamless – scan any one of six forms of personal identification, verify identity and walk away with a fully activated card in hand. With this model, GoTyme is signing up 10,000 customers a day to reach a significant milestone of 5 million customers in just over two years since its launch in October 2022. Attention to customer experience in-store helps entrench customer loyalty, including dedicated cashier lanes for clients to cash in or cash out, 'barkers' who promote the brand in-store, and a loyalty programme that gives up to three-times GoRewards to GoTyme card users.

And then, with the greatest possible signalling to potential customers in the Philippines, the highly respected Lance Gokongwei himself became a GoTyme card user. It wasn't just a symbolic gesture – he actively uses the card, testing its functionality, experiencing the in-store customer journey first-hand and reinforcing his belief in the model. This hands-on approach sends a strong message: GoTyme isn't just another digital bank; it is deeply integrated into the Gokongwei Group's retail ecosystem, and it is built to serve customers where they already shop, spend and transact.

Partnering solves a swathe of CAGE challenges in one go. On-the-ground presence dissolves physical distance. Local skin in the game brings cultural affiliation. Embedded institutional knowledge leapfrogs the arduous and expensive task of getting to grips with administrative burdens.

In some ways, this partnership replicated the successful South African partnership model established with the Pick n Pay Group, Boxer Limited and The Foschini Group.

Thinking in terms of the CAGE framework demands difficult balancing acts. Proximity versus scale is a critical one. How far are we willing to go for access to a large population? Here digital banking has an advantage over industries with big logistical footprints. With branches in the cloud, moving is relatively easy. In digital banking, the pursuit of scale can evidently override traditional considerations of market proximity.[10]

Then there is growth. Recall the powerful synergy between the economy and company performance. The Southeast Asian markets are among the fastest-growing digital economies globally. In 2021, just ahead of Tyme's expansion to the Philippines, the region's internet economy reached approximately US$174 billion in gross merchandise value (GMV). And this was projected to more than double to reach US$360 billion by 2025. The digital economy is expected to continue to grow in the region of 15% year-on-year, measured by GMV.[11] The Philippine economy is well positioned to benefit from important economic reforms.[12] As one of the more economically open countries in the Southeast Asian region, the Philippines has the potential to capitalise on enhanced logistics and trade facilitation, which would boost cross-border transactions and stimulate growth. Moreover, the country's push to improve economic complexity – by investing in high-quality education and fostering job-market alignment – signals a commitment to sustaining productivity gains. This combination of openness, economic reform and digital expansion makes the Philippines an attractive market for digital financial services.

Shern Teo, GoTyme's chief strategy and proposition officer, also highlights the importance of a supportive and progressive regulatory environment. Crucially, the Philippines' regulatory ecosystem is increasingly geared towards enabling innovation in digital banking.[13] The BSP has taken significant steps to foster this environment through a progressive regulatory framework. In 2023, it introduced key reforms aimed at balancing technological advancement with financial stability and consumer protection, notably revising e-money regulations to enhance risk management and strengthen consumer safeguards. The BSP also released guidelines for digital marketplace models, allowing banks and e-money issuers to integrate diverse financial services into digital platforms.

Additionally, the BSP has strengthened customer due diligence protocols by incorporating electronic Know Your Customer (e-KYC) processes, which streamline onboarding while upholding robust anti-money laundering controls. Another notable feature of the regulatory environment is the BSP's allowance for data hosting outside of the country – an important enabler of the unit economics that underpin Tyme's digital banking model. These initiatives reflect a serious regulatory commitment to building a secure, efficient and inclusive digital financial ecosystem. For GoTyme, this represents a hospitable and enabling environment.

But an enabling environment is only as effective as the operating model that responds to it. This is where Tyme's approach to internal execution stands out, particularly in an area many see as dry or bureaucratic: risk management.

Even on the mundane task of risk management, Tyme has a unique approach. 'Under the Commonwealth Bank of Australia, 60 people were involved in managing and mitigating risk. In building GoTyme, two people were involved in risk, three in compliance and one in internal audit,' explains Josam Watson, interim GoTyme chief risk officer and Tyme Group chief risk officer.

'There is a risk that a team of six is seen as lightweights,' Watson acknowledges, 'but this isn't the case as risk management is everyone's task, and we achieve this by having everyone understand and assess it using a common framework. Risk is everyone's business in day-to-day management, and it is integral to our process.

'A really good measure of how you're doing is culture. An effective risk management system is one where issues are brought to the surface quickly and are dealt with and resolved with root cause analysis at the heart of the resolution.

'Questions that we need to ask include: what is the problem? Do we understand the root cause? How do we fix it? In following up, have we solved it? And inside of the group, never finger-pointing or recriminations. Among most other banks, risk is late in the process – after strategy, innovation, finance, etc. In the Philippines, risk was at the start of the process, involved in the application for the bank licence,' says Watson.

Another consideration in country selection is digital adoption and penetration. High smartphone penetration and digital payment adoption create fertile ground for digital banking services. By the time Tyme entered the country, the Philippines had made notable strides in smartphone penetration, standing at 64.96% in 2022 and rising to 68.44% in 2023.[14] This positioned the Philippines among countries with significant smartphone usage. Digital payments had also seen substantial growth. In 2023, digital payments accounted for 52.8% of total retail transactions, surpassing the BSP's target of 50%.[15] This increase reflects a broader shift towards digital financial services in the country. And while the Philippines has made significant progress, there is still room for growth in smartphone penetration and digital payment adoption, offering rich opportunity in digital banking.

The Philippine banking industry is characterised by a diverse range of financial institutions: 45 universal and commercial banks, 44 savings banks, 400 rural and cooperative banks, 40 credit unions and over 6,200 non-banks with quasi-banking functions. Yet a few large banks dominate the industry, giving a concentration ratio of 66.3%. This indicates moderate concentration, which has been steadily rising over the last 15 years.[16]

More than its concentration, what defines the sector is its age – many of the country's leading banks have been around for over a century. Institutions like the Bank of the Philippine Islands (founded in 1851) and the Philippine National Bank (established in 1916) are deeply entrenched, delivering an anaemic return on equity in the region of 10% – poor by global standards. This shaped a financial system that, while stable, moves at an almost glacial pace. Teo spoke at length about an industry made up of 'sleeping giants' with little innovation, poor credit bureau data and almost no access to lending.

The 5-6 lending system is the shadow side of the Philippines' slow, oligopolised banking sector. A ruthless but accessible form of microcredit that thrives where formal finance fails, in the 5-6 system, you borrow five pesos today, repay six pesos 'soon' – a 20% interest rate, often collected daily or weekly. No paperwork, no collateral, just relentless, high-cost liquidity for small business owners and cash-strapped individuals. Although technically illegal, 5-6 lenders remain entrenched, filling the gaps left by sluggish banks and rigid loan requirements. While government programmes aim to replace them, in a system where speed matters more than legality, the 5-6 network remains a lifeline for many – and an opportunity for Tyme to step in and challenge the sluggish, egregious structure.[17]

In late 2024 Tyme deepened its commitment to the Philippines by acquiring SAVii – the country's largest fintech salary lender. As Teo put it, this move was 'another piece in an increasingly impressive jigsaw puzzle', expanding Tyme's reach into the credit space and strengthening its position in the broader financial ecosystem.

Thoroughly convinced that the Philippines made perfect sense, we asked Jonker an extension question: where to next? He didn't miss a beat.

'Indonesia.'

GoTyme: Next stop, Jakarta

Growth often means expanding across borders. Nubank took a more conventional approach to internationalisation. They expanded within Latin America. Tyme's leap from South Africa to the Philippines and then to Indonesia was a calculated deviation from the rules. It broke across lines of longitude, time zones, languages and other significant barriers.

Looking at each move more closely gives clues about Tyme's approach to expansion. The jump to the Philippines took a more expected approach of targeting deposits and transactions first. That forms the basis for more complex banking functions – lending and beyond. The Indonesian expansion is flipping that. They are starting with lending.

PART IV: THE SECOND TYME

'Most digital banks will seek to build a deposit base first and then execute their lending strategy after. What that does ... is it digs a bit of a hole,' explains John Kane, Tyme's CEO of Merchant Cash Advance for Asia. 'Tyme's new model [entering with Merchant Cash Advance as the first product], on the other hand, allows for faster profitability.'[18]

This expedited move directly to more profitable banking activity is enabled by a partnership. Tyme is working with Finfra, a lending infrastructure firm, through its subsidiary DanaBijak. This means the licensing and regulatory backend is already in place. GoTyme Indonesia can focus on making the lending work.

There is another special feature to their partnering approach. Tyme's Indonesia strategy involves being more than just a lender. It will inject an element of partnership with growing businesses. Marketing-Interactive reports, 'By tying its success directly to the performance of its partners, Tyme is betting on the ability of local businesses to thrive and expand. In this sense, Tyme isn't just hoping to boost its own revenue – it's working to help its partners boost theirs.'[19]

As Tim Delahunty, CEO and director of GoTyme Indonesia, puts it, 'We are very confident that we will be able to achieve a win-win-win outcome for our partners, for our merchants and ourselves.'[20]

Andrew Tan sums up the challenge in Indonesia. 'For Tyme, Indonesia is likely to be a much tougher market to enter with regulatory risk and uncertainty. The choice of partner is critical to success, and the market comes with specific challenges, for example, high levels of non-performing loans. Mainstream banks will likely retaliate, too. Add in geopolitical risk. As with Southeast Asia generally, balancing speed and scale, while managing strength and stability, KYC and anti-money laundering are all critical.'

The end-game in Indonesia is to build a full-service digital bank, like Tyme is doing in South Africa and the Philippines. Already the path to that goal in Indonesia is unfolding differently, highlighting the need for flexibility across new markets.

Chapter 12

Back from the Edge

One must imagine Sisyphus happy.
— Albert Camus

Jonker and the king

'Isn't this all a bit overambitious?' we asked. It was late afternoon, and we were meeting with Coen Jonker in Tyme's Cape Town office in Woodstock. 'Isn't it a little crazy? Like that business school metaphor of building a plane while you're flying, except your pilot is also riding a bicycle?' Jonker's wry retort: 'Yes. Almost. But in this case, the pilot is also juggling skittles – and it's a unicycle that he's riding.'

Nic Smalle, from the London-based private equity fund Apis Partners, an investor in Tyme, positions Jonker's approach without sugar sprinkles. 'Coen is excessively optimistic – it is his strength and his weakness. I don't think you would have done this if you were not excessively optimistic. To build this you must be obsessed.' Smalle reflects, 'But, if we had known then what we know now, we would have invested even more.'

The plane, skittles and unicycle in question included at least three grand projects: the ongoing build of the two banks in South Africa and the Philippines by TymeX and the rebranding of TymeBank in South Africa to align with GoTyme. All three were bold and gutsy, with enough risk to make the average executive want to lie down in a dark room.

'You're missing a project,' says Jonker. 'For us to rebrand in South Africa

PART IV: THE SECOND TYME

we must also build a new banking app to ensure the customer experience matches … no, exceeds … their expectations under the new brand. And TymeX is responsible for that build also.'

This is no cosmetic overhaul, either. In early 2025, Raymund Villanueva, a GoTyme executive from Manila, relocated to Cape Town to become chief marketing officer of TymeBank, where he was promptly handed the task of repositioning the brand for a new era. Or, as he put it with typical understatement, 'painting the South African bank Tiffany Blue from top to toe'. Dieter Botha sums up the challenge. 'In the Philippines, GoTyme is an aspirational brand,' he says. 'Whereas TymeBank in South Africa has been seen as "a poor man's bank".' Nobody wants to feel like they're in the 'poor' target market.

Jonker's comfort with the seemingly impossible can be baffling, but it looks good on him. 'For a business with our ambition – to build a multi-country bank that champions inclusion and innovation is a modern-day Sisyphean task,' he quips.

In the ancient Greek myth, Sisyphus is the king condemned by the gods to eternally push a boulder up a mountain, only for it to roll back down each time he nears the summit. Jonker's description of TymeBank's mission as Sisyphean might seem like an admission of futility, or, at least, a miserable grind. That's not how he sees it.

French philosopher Albert Camus put it best in his seminal work, *The Myth of Sisyphus*. Camus frames the king's endless struggle, devoid of victory or escape, as the perfect metaphor for the human experience. But not as a tale of pain or punishment. Rather, he argues, 'The struggle itself towards the heights is enough to fill a man's heart.' In other words, Sisyphus isn't miserable. According to Camus, at least, Sisyphus is living the dream because happiness lies not in reaching the summit but in the act of pushing, in embracing the absurdity of his fate and choosing to find meaning within it.

'Each setback – a regulatory hurdle, a technological misfire, a market that does not respond as predicted – can feel like the boulder rolling back down the hill,' says Jonker. 'But, like Camus' *Sisyphus*, we find purpose not just in the destination but in the climb.' For Tyme, each failed initiative, each hard-won lesson, is not a defeat but a necessary part of the ascent. This belief – that the reward lies in effort, not outcome – comes naturally to Jonker. Winningly, he follows this grand philosophical statement with a touch of self-deprecation. 'We also create our own boulders and steeper hills.'

Angela Duckworth's work on grit, the mix of perseverance and passion for long-term goals, has earned widespread acclaim.[1] She argues success is more about sustained effort than talent. Tyme proves her point. The business has pushed through setbacks, recalibrations and relentless pursuit. Its progress is the result of persistence, not overnight triumph.

Which brings us back to those four projects – none of them accidental, and all of them weight-bearing in the broader strategy. In digital banking, the real threat is not competition or regulation. It is complacency. Pushing the limits is not a rarity. It is your daily grind. 'If we don't feel we stand a good chance of failure,' says Jonker, 'then we're not taking on hard enough challenges.'

It is not false modesty. He and his team have options. They could slow down. Coast. No one would fault them. But they won't. 'We have to stay fit,' Jonker says. 'Our edge isn't in the tech stack – not really. It's in our ability to move faster than the rest. Digital banking is about price-to-performance. Our advantage is in velocity, in customer experience and in the passion that gives people agency to live their best lives.'

The grit of Jonker and Van der Walt is quiet but extreme. Neither boasts about long hours and sacrifice like it is a badge of honour. But sleeping at the office and working through the night happens when necessary.

Enter stage left: TymeX.

TymeX: A Vietnamese coding powerhouse

So, what then, of TymeX – the expansive Vietnamese coding outfit tasked with building a global bank, line of code by precise line of painstakingly crafted code?

To find out, we travelled to Ho Chi Minh City, or HCMC – formerly

Saigon, for the Boomers out there. It is a natural home for TymeX: fast-growing, outward-facing and increasingly the beating heart of Vietnam's tech scene. The city runs on motorbikes, instant noodles and computer code. From the colonial boulevards of District 1 to the steel-and-glass of the Saigon Hi-Tech Park, the atmosphere is unmistakable: young, caffeinated and permanently in motion.

We arrived at the Lumiere Riverside office just before Tet, the Vietnamese Lunar New Year, and spent the better part of a week with the TymeX team, engaging in a dozen interviews, closer to two dozen meals with the team, many cups of coffee, and an evening riding through the city on scooters. Fittingly, that night ended in Bui Vien, Saigon's 'never-sleep' street. It was there, somewhere between a street vendor and a thumping bassline, that the metaphor came full circle: a team moving quickly, carrying a heavy load and still smiling.

The structure of this unusual function resembles something Henry Ford would have admired: an assembly line for banks. TymeX is not a bank itself. It is a factory that manufactures banks at scale. Process by process, it broke the business of banking into components that could be improved, rebuilt or shipped out like a chassis.

On its website, TymeX describes itself, with some flourish, as 'the next-gen technology engine powering Tyme Group's banking around the world by developing reusable assets that are constantly optimised and can be easily replicated across our countries, enabling our banks to be built and scaled rapidly across the globe'. It's a long sentence. But the underlying idea is simple: build once, deploy repeatedly.[2]

TymeX's first offices in Saigon reflected that same commitment to speed and function – albeit with little evidence of glamour. As part of our visit to HCMC, we were taken on a timeline tour of TymeX's office addresses. Our guide was Quynh Ngo, part of Tyme's first team in Vietnam, and today TymeX's finance controller. At our first stop, she took us up to the sixth floor of an old city building to see the workspace: 15 square metres that had been crammed with 13 coders and developers – and a request from Ngo to step over a dead mouse on the way into the building. On the sixth floor, the kitchen was a one-at-a-time affair, and the toilet was within arm's reach of at least one of the desks, perhaps two desks. The visit to the first office highlights the grit and hustle of TymeX's early days and captures the spirit of a company that turned scrappy beginnings into a platform for global success.

The space had the audacity of P.T. Barnum, or a Musk-era factory walk-through: a show of something that didn't fully exist – yet. The set builders weren't conning anyone. They were revealing belief. A mock-up not of what Tyme had, but what it would become.

It is tempting to assume that the Vietnamese operation was born of visionary thinking. It had more to do with luck and problem-solving than foresight and savvy. The truth is, when TymeBank's South African team of developers walked out for another opportunity in 2017, it left the bank high and dry. Fortunately, Tyme's shareholder at the time, the Commonwealth Bank of Australia (CBA), had a solution. Leveraging its Southeast Asian footprint, CBA provided a small team of coders and developers in Vietnam, charged with supporting a 'new project'.

Ngo was one of those 'first responders' sent by CBA. She joined TymeX as part of the finance team, despite knowing almost nothing about digital banking. CBA's involvement brought improvements in accommodation and an upgraded address. But the stay at the smarter real estate in the Riverfront Financial Centre was relatively short-lived – a casualty of CBA's convulsion and divestment of Tyme.

In 2018, when TymeBank was sold back to the founders and African Rainbow Capital (ARC), and the founders and the team were forced to cut costs to the bone. This included relocating to a nearby university building to save money. The single elevator – shared with university students – carried the TymeX team up 19 floors to an open workspace without air-conditioning, where summer temperatures hovered around 37 degrees Celsius, with 85% relative humidity. Sisyphean conditions, one might say, survived only with a spirit that would make Jonker proud.

TymeX is a franchisor. It designs and runs the systems that power TymeBank in South Africa and GoTyme in the Philippines – systems that look similar on the outside but have been carefully calibrated for their respective markets. TymeX delivers BaaS – Banking as a Service – not as a consultancy or outsourced dev shop, but as a strategic core. Its new headquarters sit in Lumiere Riverside, one of Ho Chi Minh City's newer mixed-use developments. The office, much like the business, is modern, vertical and quietly ambitious. HCMC, for its part, is rapidly becoming Southeast Asia's fintech sandbox – fast, fluid and not yet burdened by the legacies of older markets. Think Silicon Valley, but at a fraction of the cost.

Officially, TymeX's mandate is to maintain and evolve the platforms for two active banks – one in Johannesburg, the other in Manila – while simultaneously building MultiX: a modular, plug-and-play banking platform designed to cross borders without fuss. Think of it as a Lego Creator set. It has all the blocks a digital bank needs. Each new jurisdiction demands much the same selection of blocks, just assembled differently to meet local laws and regulations. And if the Lego piece doesn't exist, TymeX has the skill to create the custom piece at scale and with speed.

Who does that?

An extraordinary thing like TymeX doesn't get done by ordinary people. Dieter Botha is no ordinary fintech engineer. He holds the titles of CEO of TymeX and group chief technology officer for the Tyme Group – roles that place him at the centre of both strategy and system.

Botha studied BCom in Accounting at Rhodes University in the Eastern Cape. By pure coincidence, he was resident in the same university residence as one of this book's authors. His work resumé is formidable, including leadership roles at high-profile institutions like CBA, Oracle and the Standard Bank Group. By the time he joined Tyme in late 2018, just as TymeBank was preparing to go live, he was a seasoned operator with the rare distinction of understanding both the plumbing and the poetry of digital banking.

During our conversations, Botha laid out how the industry has shifted and why TymeX has managed to keep pace where others have not. Banking, he says, is still a tough business. But the nature of the toughness has changed. Where once it was about 'sweating assets' – squeezing more from branches, servers and balance sheets – today it is about tending an ecosystem. 'It's no longer just a machine,' he says. 'It's a garden. You're grooming an ever-moving network of partners, platforms and parts. That's banking in 2025.'

The list of these parts reads like a modern CIO's toolbelt: Amazon Web Services for cloud hosting, Apple's iOS for mobile environments, Confluence and Miro for collaborative product design, Slack for internal communication, and even Eskom APIs for integrating with South Africa's electricity system. The old model of capital expenditure – heavy upfront investment in infrastructure – has been traded for a nimbler operating expenditure approach. TymeX scales not by building, but by plugging in.

The result is a system that runs fast and light. By adopting an ecosystem approach, TymeX has converted 'capex' into 'opex' – swapping big upfront costs like buying servers or building branches for a more flexible, pay-as-you-go model. This structure allows TymeX to scale up or down instantly, ensuring the business remains agile and responsive to changing demands.

Data is distributed across three sites, ensuring resilience, robust backup, regulatory compliance and disaster recovery. Out of this distributed data ecosystem, TymeX gathers more than 10 billion customer events per month, creating a powerful, self-reinforcing system. These customer events fall into two broad categories: transactional events and behavioural events, which strengthen system security, deliver vital information and build customer insights. Transactional events are the everyday actions customers take – like buying coffee at Starbucks, topping up airtime or purchasing a Lotto ticket. They represent straightforward financial transactions that occur continuously throughout the day. Behavioural events provide deeper insights into how customers interact with TymeX's systems. Every interaction, from tapping the bank icon to opening the app, entering a PIN or Face ID, scrolling through pages, or swiping the app away, generates a data point. The system even captures subtle metrics, such as the angle at which a user holds their phone through the device's accelerometer – which happens to know if you're a left-handed or right-handed user, and this enhances the security and the richness of the behavioural profile. Billions of these behavioural events stream live into TymeX's systems, helping the company understand customer habits, improve products and enhance marketing efforts. Within the system, all customer data is anonymised except on frontend servicing, where customer identity is required for customer engagement. The business is operated on European Union data privacy standards.

More importantly, these behavioural signals feed into fraud AI models, augmenting traditional controls like PINs and device fingerprinting. By building detailed behavioural profiles, TymeX continually strengthens its ability to detect anomalies and keep customers' money safe. This dynamic and adaptive data ecosystem not only powers security but also drives innovation, learning and product refinement – creating a self-reinforcing model that grows stronger with every interaction.

This should evidence that speed on its own is not the point – not entirely. 'The ambition,' Botha says, 'is to build a bank that delivers exceptional customer experience and exceptional efficiency.' His definition of efficiency is more granular than most: measured in milliseconds per transaction and dollars per customer.

By those metrics, the bank delivers. Cost of customer acquisition sits at just US$5. Operating cost per customer: US$7 per year. The bank's net promoter score in the Philippines outpaces its competitors by 10 to 15 points. The fact that the mobile app scores 4.5 in Apple's App Store – a rating more commonly associated with food-delivery apps than financial institutions – is nevertheless another indicator of excellence.

And yet, for Botha, that is not enough. The standard is not 'done' – it is 'better'. TymeX pursues what it calls constant business value improvements: fewer bugs, lower risk, more resilience and a better customer experience. 'Better, sooner, safer,' he says of the three-word philosophy that guides the team's daily release cadence.

That cadence is relentless. TymeX rolls out up to 30 code improvements a day, every day. For most banks, the traditional South African holiday period from mid-December to mid-January is a time to freeze new developments, minimise risk and pray nothing breaks. Botha rolls his eyes at the convention. 'Freezing is for the weak,' he says. At TymeX, the systems do not freeze – they flex. Agility is not a goal. It is the superpower. And they have the numbers to prove it.

'TymeX is not a bank', says Botha. 'And so the people building the business are not bankers. Forget about the balance sheet; TymeX is the engine of the group. We are leaders in tech but do not sell tech; we are a scale competitor, not a niche player; we are customer obsessed; and we are a single business, not a conglomerate.'

So, what is TymeX? Botha describes it as a 'fintech hub'. The coders and engineers that make up the TymeX team could just as easily be developing a gaming platform or a delivery app, he says. TymeX's product – or service – just happens to be banking.

It is not just the tech that sets Tyme apart. Its global workforce is another feature more commonly associated with Silicon Valley-style startups than traditional banking. Botha has a playful take on the Tyme acronym (Take Your Money Everywhere) to 'Take Your Team Everywhere'. It is apt. Tyme has team members in Vietnam, the Philippines, Portugal, Germany, Singapore, Hong Kong, India, New Zealand, South Africa, the US, the UK and Indonesia – with more locations to come. Spanning 18 time zones, Tyme never stops.

Botha talks about the rare sense of pragmatism at Tyme that creates a fundamentally different operating environment. He singles out Owen Sorour, TymeBank's chief risk officer, as an example. 'He has nothing to prove,' says Botha, and that makes all the difference. Sorour is not focused on protecting his own career. He is all about results – what is best for the bank and its clients. 'That's not always the case at other banks, and it gives much deeper purpose to the task of building banking systems.' In making this point about Sorour, it seems like Botha could be talking about an individual who represents the ethos and character of the group.

Quan Nguyen Hoang, director of engineering at TymeX, adds colour to Botha's comment on culture: 'While traditional banks are steeped in legacy systems and rigid hierarchies, tech companies like Tyme thrive on curiosity and innovation.' Hoang has embedded this mindset in his team with an idea he picked up from James Clear's book *Atomic Habits*, which he actively encourages his team to read.³ Once a week, TymeX's book club meets to share their learnings from books on productivity, leadership, psychology, management, innovation and other relevant topics.

It is an approach backed by evidence-based research, which shows that a culture of learning is a key attribute that separates winning businesses from the rest.⁴ It is especially valuable in Vietnam, where the education system is strong in building technical capability: Vietnam ranks 10th globally, producing approximately 100,000 engineering graduates annually.⁵ But the country's graduates are not as strong in broader skills like critical thinking and teamwork – both of which are prized at Tyme. That sense of engagement feeds into something bigger. The team's reading habit fosters a curious, challenger mindset that is not just at odds with old-school banking culture, but also runs counter to Vietnam's more hierarchical management style.

Hoang cites a benefit he had not anticipated. The book club has boosted retention. 'People feel a strong sense of membership,' he says. 'It isn't that hard to leave a job. But nobody wants to leave a place where you feel like you belong and matter.' That is a weighty competitive advantage in a game where engineering talent is highly sought after.

A LeSS peg for a round hole

Understandably, then, Tyme's workplace culture is an awkward fit for Vietnam. This was especially the case in the early days of the firm's involvement, where TymeBank, the principal client – six hours away by time zone, at least 18 hours by plane, and a very large distance by CAGE miles – was an unknown.

'We were not equipped or prepared culturally to operate to the demands of the management framework that was adopted,' explains Hoang. An example of this divide lies in Craig Larman and Bas Vodde's Large-Scale Scrum (LeSS) model. Brought over from the South African operation, this is characterised by simplicity, decentralisation and a strong focus on customer value through iterative development.⁶

Unlike traditional management approaches that rely on control, hierarchy and rigid processes, which would feel far more natural to a Vietnamese team, LeSS encourages managers to take a step back. Instead of calling the shots, they act as guides or coaches, helping teams work independently and make their own decisions. This shift demands trust, collaboration and openness – a tough ask in Vietnam, where respect for authority and top-down decision-making are the norm. The cultural instinct to avoid confrontation and keep the peace also made it difficult for teams to have the kind of candid back-and-forth communication that LeSS demands. To deliver, TymeX needs to deliver reliably at speed – and LeSS puts this on the table. But getting the TymeX coders and engineers to work this way didn't exactly take off.

Always be yourself unless you can be Batman
Then along came Chris Bennett, who joined TymeX from CBA in December 2018. His job title? LinkedIn confirms it: 'Batman'. That alone gives you a sense of the management-style shakeup that was about to happen. Bennett presented a clear call to action: 'Let's fix this.' What followed was a relentless push to shift the culture towards agile teams with accountable leads – people empowered to speak up, move fast and take risks to get the LeSS system from a concept into action.

Daily morning meetings are one manifestation of the company culture. Tuan Bui, director of engineering, says the team runs an adrenaline-shot meeting to discuss what happened yesterday on every front and each product, what changes went in overnight, what worked, what didn't – and why. These meetings also reflect Botha's philosophy that building a complex system is a social endeavour.

In implementing LeSS, one of the challenges Bennett faced was that the Vietnamese team was not comfortable making mistakes. This made it difficult for them to learn and adapt quickly. To tackle this problem, they were urged, in Botha's words, to 'move fast and embarrass themselves'. Mistakes weren't punished but expected. It was cultural whiplash, but it worked. 'Botha has made this a safe place for failure,' says Vin Le.

As part of the bid to make failure sexy, TymeX introduced the Chuck

PART IV: THE SECOND TYME

Mungh Award – named after the Vietnamese for 'celebrate'. The fortnightly award recognises people for 'just trying and often messing up', says Botha. It is an expression of his belief that failure is not just acceptable but essential.

Botha's approach echoes the lessons of some of history's most successful innovators. Thomas Edison famously stated, 'I have not failed. I've just found 10,000 ways that won't work.' His relentless experimentation was built on the belief that each setback brought him closer to a breakthrough. Soichiro Honda, founder of Honda Motor Co., shared a similar mindset: 'Success represents the 1% of your work which results from the 99% that is called failure.' Their stories highlight a truth Botha understands well: that greatness doesn't come from avoiding mistakes but from embracing them as essential stepping stones.

Adam Grant, the organisational psychologist, reinforces this point. He argues that true progress and innovation often depend on a willingness to fail repeatedly. 'If you want to hit the target, you must be willing to miss,' Grant writes.[7] Whether it's Edison, Honda or TymeX's Chuck Mungh Award, the lesson is the same: progress rarely follows a straight line. What matters is not avoiding failure but learning from it.

Companies like Google and Tata have long recognised failure as a driver of success. Google's moonshot factory, X, holds regular 'failure parties', where teams openly share what didn't work and, more importantly, what they learnt. Similarly, the Tata Group introduced the 'Dare to Try' Award, honouring the best failed ideas across its conglomerate. In each case, the goal is the same: change the way employees think to foster an environment of innovation.

John F. Kennedy knew the benefit of a culture that embraced owning your errors. He once said, 'Victory has a hundred fathers, but defeat is an orphan.' He used the line in the aftermath of the Bay of Pigs fiasco, when no one wanted to claim responsibility. It wasn't originally his – Napoleon and Tacitus said it earlier – but Kennedy delivered it with the kind of weary grace that made it stick.

While TymeX may not have invented the wheel, the celebration of failure is emblematic of their ability to intelligently break a status quo. If setbacks are fuel for learning, then Tyme has plenty of material to work with. 'It is not about what you know,' concludes Tauriq Keraan, former CEO of TymeBank South Africa. 'It's about what you learn.'

Trials and tribulations: Your worst moment in Tyme

In each meeting, we asked members of the TymeX team: 'What was your worst moment in Tyme?' Several people gave the same answer: 16 December 2021. The day the TymeBank system went down. For a bank – anywhere, anytime – this is the nightmare scenario. Like waking up to find the floor has disappeared beneath your feet. Bui explains: 'I personally felt useless, and we owed the customers a million apologies.'

When the crisis hit, the mood was what Bui describes as 'calm panic'. Cool heads presided over adrenaline-fuelled chaos as the team scrambled to figure out what had gone wrong. It turned out the extremely busy holiday period in South Africa had caused a system overload. The outage triggered a vicious loop: customers whose transactions weren't being processed were making repeated attempts – a snowballing effect – and then were accessing their accounts through their apps to process transactions. This ballooning of activity put the system into a spiral, which only increased the strain on the system. The fix required shutting the system down momentarily to add computing horsepower from the cloud, and the vertical scaling of the system enabled a restart. With huge relief, Bui saw the first green blip. The first customer was back online. More followed as customers were slowly fed back into the system. The system shutdown may not have been eligible for the Chuck Mungh Award – that award is for small mistakes that cause big 'ahas'. This was a bigger mistake that causes an even bigger 'aha' – and with the additional computing horsepower, the system worked seamlessly through the busy holiday period and into the new year. But the outcome of the incident – and lesser incidents that fall under the Chuck Mungh Award – is a cultural determination to learn. As the system recovered, 'crisis' became 'calm' became 'experience'. Patches can be cultural as well as technological.

PART IV: THE SECOND TYME

But nightmares sometimes return, with variations on scenes, characters or settings. In June 2023, GoTyme went down in the Philippines. Bui's nightmare became Bennett's worst moment at Tyme. As during the 2021 outage, the team went into triage, scouring the system for the root cause. The culprit was an SSL certificate that sits behind every web address – in this case gotyme.com.ph – that had not been renewed.[8] The SSL certificate had expired on the back of a payment that had failed. And the payment had failed because the credit card that was used to set up the certificate had expired. It was a personal card that had been used to make payment for the certificate in the early days of Tyme. 'This was really embarrassing,' says Bennett. A mom 'n pop laundry would find this a silly error. But it could have been worse.

Once the SSL certificate was renewed, the bank was back up and running, and the whole drama was resolved in an hour and 55 minutes – just five minutes shy of the two-hour threshold, at which point GoTyme would have to report the outage to the regulator. That would have been a different kind of lesson.

They were not the first successful scale-up to trip over a legacy glitch from the startup days, and they won't be the last. Jonker, of course, sees the learnings in this failure. When a business scales up, he says, one of the tasks is to go back and find the Rube Goldberg problems. Goldberg's cartoons feature gizmos and contraptions of exaggerated complexity, over-designed to perform comedically simple tasks in the most elaborate way imaginable.

But what about the best days in Tyme? Anthony Blackie, portfolio product manager based in HCMC, describes his best day as the onboarding of Customer #1: Bongani Maponya. Now the managing executive of value segment at TymeBank, Maponya was a junior accountant at the time. Blackie becomes quite animated (for an engineer), saying, 'Actually, I have a lot of good days here. And the best days are when the team delivers something that was considered impossible. I love it. I am so proud of them.' And if that doesn't reflect the boundary-pushing, ever-striving, failure-embracing culture of Tyme, then nothing will. Perhaps we were witnessing another of those best days when we met with Tess Bach, who oversees

TymeX's product teams. During our meeting, Bach's delight was palpable as she shared some significant news: TikTok had just appointed TymeX to build a merchant cash advance solution tailored to its Southeast Asian sellers. The announcement was delivered quietly but carried enormous weight. It marked yet another vote of confidence in TymeX – this time, from a global tech titan.

Each time they fall short, TymeX edges them closer to success. And this gives them the courage to pursue what others in the industry regard as impossible: MultiX.

The MultiX ambition: Building the banking platform of the future

Sure, TymeX is meeting the Sisyphean challenge of developing world-class code for its banks in the Philippines and South Africa. But that is not enough. It has another grand ambition: to build MultiX.

MultiX is Tyme's plan to become 'a single, integrated, global business' that can move 'from one country to the next faster, faster and faster'.[9] 'MultiX is a way of bringing it all together,' says Karl Westvig, TymeBank CEO, 'so that we have best practice across all the territories ... a common set of tools, a common set of products, and a common set of propositions', all united under a single brand. But the real goal (as the name suggests) is rapid scalability.

In theory, MultiX allows Tyme to build digital banks like a production line – taking what works in one country and quickly adapting it for another. The idea is simple: build once, use everywhere. Assets will be designed to be replicable or reusable so that when Tyme moves into new markets, it isn't starting from scratch. It is like a mothership that can spawn a new bank-in-a-box to be adapted and deployed in any country, fast.

Additionally, the MultiX strategy emphasises 'MultiX as a Service' (XaaS) – a model that would give product teams self-service capabilities to build features without waiting for platform team support. This means faster product development, more innovation and lower costs. It is a smart, scalable system that could allow TymeX to deliver banking solutions to emerging markets quickly and competitively.

PART IV: THE SECOND TYME

It is a unique vision. While Revolut and N26, by way of example, have built multi-country banks, they have done so within essentially a single-currency system under one regulator. TymeX aims for something far more ambitious: building a truly cross-border, cross-currency, cross-regulatory bank – a feat with no clear precedent.

So, what would it look like if TymeX could pull off this grand ambition? Jonker believes it could become one of the largest and most successful multi-country digital banks in the world. Westvig continues, 'Once you've got a common set of platforms, it allows you to open a new territory quickly. Whereas it took South Africa three years to open the bank, and 12 months in the Philippines, this could mean we open a bank in six months.'

Botha notes that MultiX should bring down costs for customers in both existing and new territories, while building a better-quality customer experience. David Pfaff, co-CEO at Tyme Group, goes further in noting that not only will MultiX make the group more resilient but also more profitable. And Nate Clarke, CEO of GoTyme Bank, completes the vision: 'The thing that I dream about is that when we talk to our grandkids about Tyme, we will be on the same playing field as the Citibank and other giant banks of generations before.'

While there is broad agreement among the TymeX team that the MultiX dream will become a reality, the risks have not gone unnoticed. 'We could end up with a portfolio of ten banks, eight of them duds,' notes Botha. He goes on: 'In the meantime, if resources and attention get stretched too thin, our successful banks in South Africa and the Philippines could take a hit. Growth could slow. Competitors could seize the moment. And the shareholders might lose patience.'

Risks aside, there is plenty to figure out before forging ahead. For one thing, if you are going to replicate something repeatedly, your blueprint better be flawless. Botha is clear that TymeBank is not the right starting point. 'It's not what you want to repeat. It was version 1.0. However, the Philippines is replicable. It is version 2.0, and we should build 2.1 in Indonesia, and perhaps 2.2 in Vietnam.' There is also a third option: start from scratch.

That is exactly what fintech giant Grab Holdings has done. A leading Southeast Asian technology company, Grab is best known for its super app, which offers everything from ride-hailing to food delivery and financial services. Its digital banking arm, GXS Bank – a joint venture with Singtel – operates in Singapore and Malaysia, focusing on underserved segments like gig economy workers and small businesses, with digital-first solutions such as savings accounts, microloans and payment services.

Grab's initial challenge was integrating digital banking services into its existing ecosystem. They came up against inflexible infrastructure, data silos and integration issues. The legacy technology stack struggled to meet modern banking requirements, particularly around security, compliance and the seamless flow of financial data. The result was predictable: a clunky user experience, limited scalability and rising costs. In short, trying to retrofit a digital bank into a legacy system generated technical debt, elevated costs and amplified operational risks.

So Grab took a different path – it started fresh. It adopted a greenfield approach: designing and deploying an entirely new technology stack, free from legacy constraints. This allowed engineers to select best-in-class tools, architectures and development frameworks, rather than being locked into outdated systems or forced to maintain backward compatibility. It also enabled Grab to move faster, iterate in real time and optimise for customer experience from day one – not as a patch, but as the foundation. Grab was building its dream home on open land instead of trying to remodel the house it inherited from its parents.

But Tyme doesn't have years to create something fresh. Westvig points out that the longer Tyme takes putting all the banks together on a single platform, the further apart they grow. Any bank that has tried this type of integration will bear testimony: Absa Group (South Africa), Bank Syariah Indonesia (Indonesia), the Consolidated Bank of Ghana (Ghana), Deutsche Bank (Germany), Emirates NBD (UAE), Mizuho Financial Group (Japan), State Bank of India (India), TSB Bank (UK) – the list is long. The sooner the integration happens, the less pain the individuals and the collective will go through, and the better the result for customers and shareholders.

Pfaff reinforces this: 'If we don't do it now, it's going to become too difficult, too complex, too costly, and take too much time.' Clarke closes out the case for MultiX: 'This must span all countries for Tyme to achieve true economies of scale. Unless that is achieved, the group will not be on a single technology platform, it won't have a single brand and Tyme won't have a single app.' For this sort of multi-country banking to work, 'it's about efficiencies and replication,' says Botha, 'and we've got to get that together now.'

Looking ahead, what does the future hold for Tyme? Bennett put it succinctly: 'Even though there's a lot of dead banks out there, I'd put the probability of complete failure for TymeX at zero. I think we crossed the threshold to zero in December 2023 when South Africa achieved profitability. That gives the business the rock on which to anchor.'

As we closed out the discussion with Jonker on TymeX, we put a final thought to him: 'To this point, your experience in growing the banks in South Africa and the Philippines have surpassed expectation. Our sense is that you've even surprised yourself.' We wondered further: 'To what extent do you think this is luck, rather than design?' Jonker didn't hesitate. 'Of course there's luck,' he said. 'But our job is to grow the surface area where luck can land.'

Chapter 13

This Tyme Is Different

The only way to make sense out of change is to plunge into it, move with it, and join the dance.
— Alan Watts

Crossing the line

Coen Jonker's frantic fundraising efforts in 2020 had the benefit of a lag effect as new investors signed up. In May 2023, two new shareholders participated in the Pre-Series C capital raise, adding Africa-focused, venture-capital fund Norrsken22, and global impact investment firm BlueEarth Capital. Tencent, which has stakes in some two dozen fintechs, opted to increase its stake and became the third biggest shareholder as a result – another valuable signal to the board at ARC that their instincts to back the business following the CBA exit had been right, despite the trials and tribulations it had brought.

In less than a year, by August 2023, GoTyme reported its one-millionth customer and, by December, TymeBank finally achieved the long-awaited goal of generating its first net monthly profit of US$340,000. For Cheslyn Jacobs, this was a seminal moment. He recalled returning from the board meeting where they had announced the breakthrough. He told his team that something had finally shifted in what had been an often-trying relationship. The board could finally relax in the knowledge that the theory could be turned into practice and Johan van Zyl could finally remove it off his 'red list' of immediate concerns. They were still some way off from delivering an annual profit but had shown they could.

TymeBank laid claim to being the fastest standalone digital bank to reach profitability in the world. It had taken Brazil's Nubank eight years and the UK's Monzo seven to reach the same. 'It was a much better board meeting,' says Jacobs. 'Finally they could see that the model could work.' At this point, fewer than 5% of digital banks in the world had reached profitability and no other digital bank in Africa was profitable.

Investors understood that as banks grow, they need new capital, as long as they can demonstrate their ability to eventually make the profit that generates the money for future growth, while rewarding shareholders with dividend flow. However, when banks are losing money, shareholders have to fund the losses. It is worse when you are growing while losing money, as shareholders get a double whammy.

Tom Boardman is philosophical about the new optimism: 'It's a very important affirmation to everybody, to the management for having stuck it out, for the board supporting the management and the shareholders for continuing to put in money.'

Was there ever a serious consideration to stop throwing good money after bad, especially during 2020 when there was no way of measuring the duration of the lockdowns and how long any recovery would take once people were able to return to work? 'There were moments of intense anxiety,' admits Boardman, 'but there was a never a suggestion of stopping. The most crucial thing to look for before joining a board is the integrity and transparency of the management team. When push comes to shove and you're a non-executive, you are only going to see what the management wants you to see, and I think because of that we had absolute confidence in them.'

Fourteen months after launch, GoTyme reported it had signed on 2.3 million customers in the Philippines, bringing the total number for the group to nearly 8.5 million. More than 200,000 people a month were opening accounts at a rate of 7,700 a day. Added into the mix was a second big acquisition – the Philippines-based payroll lender SAVii. It put Tyme in a position to start making unsecured loans available to employees in that country. In August, it began offering loans to small businesses in Indonesia. The little bank no one wanted to look at during Covid announced a bold intention to become a top-three retail bank in South Africa. Its transformation from startup to upstart was taking shape. It was starting to be recognised in prestigious awards hosted by the likes of Forbes and News24, demonstrating public recognition for its efforts.

Karl Westvig had been with the group for less than a year when Jonker offered him the role of CEO of the South Africa business. Jonker had been straddling multiple responsibilities and, as the Philippines grew and the single-digital platform took shape, he needed to be more focused on finding new opportunities for growth and preparing the business for its next audacious goal – a possible listing on a major stock exchange in 2028. He injected new discipline into what had become a sprawling South African business. He described the team, most of whom had worked closely together for a decade as 'tired and stressed out'. There were too many projects and not enough people to manage each one effectively. Tyme had always been a hotbed of ideas and experimentation, encouraged by Jonker, who thrived on pushing limits and had a propensity to say 'yes' to new ideas often.

The new CEO took a pragmatic view of the business he had inherited and immediately began slimming down its offerings and new product suites. 'We didn't need to prove innovation,' he says. 'Technology and innovation are a means to an end, and we had to bring focus back to delivering value for the customer.' He started by culling the RCS credit-card venture. It had been poorly executed and was not performing as it should. The bank had signed up too many partnerships and was generating too many licence fees for his liking. He wanted to go back to basics.

Even if he did step on toes, the simplification of the business, the reduction in the number of products and a return to a more minimalist, focused approach was welcomed. 'Ultimately we all wanted the same thing, so differences of opinion mattered less than ensuring our success,' says Westvig.

Freed from the constraints of day-to-day executive management, Jonker set his sights on a new goal – to convince the world's most successful digital bank to invest.

Chapter 14

Knighted in the Global Court of Fintech

What we call the beginning is often the end. And to make an end is to make a beginning. The end is where we start from.
— T.S. Eliot

The uncertainty of prediction

Nubank, founded in Brazil in 2013, was a digital bank trailblazer. By 2024, it was a poster child of digital banking success. Its ascent was rapid, bold and brilliant – built on the vision of three founders who came from three very different places, united by a shared discontent with the banking status quo.

David Vélez, a Colombian venture capitalist, was struck by how inefficient and anti-customer Brazil's banking system had become. After experiencing first-hand the bureaucratic nightmare of opening a bank account in São Paulo, he began sketching out what a customer-first digital bank might look like. But he needed insiders.

Cristina Junqueira was that insider. A former executive at one of Brazil's largest banks, she had grown frustrated with the industry's deep resistance to change. She had resigned from Itaú Unibanco in protest. When she met Vélez, the two instantly clicked – a rebellious banker and a visionary outsider. To complete the trio, they brought on Edward Wible, an American software engineers whose technical rigour and commitment to lean, scalable systems formed the digital backbone of Nubank.

Together, they launched from a small office in São Paulo with a single product: a zero-fee credit card powered by a mobile app. Customers loved it. Regulators didn't. And the incumbents went to war.

At the time, Brazilian credit-card issuers had up to 27 days to settle payments with merchants following a transaction. Nubank had worked out that it could make a generous margin if it managed its cash flow effectively. It had noticed that its customers typically paid off their balances in 26 days. That one-day difference created a positive cash-flow cycle, enabling it to operate without significant outside capital. It was clever, it was bold, and it worked. But the incumbents fought back. Rather than reform their own practices, they lobbied regulators to reduce the settlement period to just two days, arguing that this would benefit merchants. Had this rule been enforced, Nubank would have needed an immediate US$1-billion capital injection simply to survive. It was a near-death experience.

Junqueira was tasked with leading the fightback – something she did fiercely and with relish. She appeared on every media platform she could access, highlighting the negative consequences of the proposed change. Her voice was clear, credible and caught public attention. With mounting public support for Nubank, the central bank reverted to the original settlement terms. A fintech giant had survived its first trial by fire.

São Paulo to Southeast Asia

While Nubank was navigating regulatory landmines in Brazil, Tyme was cutting its teeth in South Africa, where four banks controlled 90% of the retail banking market. Unlike their Brazilian counterparts, however, the South African incumbents had already faced several waves of innovation. The market was competitive, technically sophisticated and fiercely defended. Tyme's founders watched Nubank's growth closely. What they saw was more than market success; it was the blueprint for how a digital bank could scale in an emerging economy. In 2019, Nubank expanded into Mexico, followed by Colombia. It became the first emerging markets digital bank to be valued at US$10 billion. Then, in December 2021, Nubank listed on the New York Stock Exchange, raising US$2.6 billion and lifting its valuation to more than US$40 billion. By the time Tyme and Nubank's leadership first met in 2023, Nubank had more than 80 million customers. Tyme's executives were watching a masterclass in execution.

A chance meeting in New York

Then, at an Endeavor conference in New York City in December 2023, a chance event presented the opportunity for Tyme's executives to meet Nubank's founders. Endeavor is a global network of high-impact entrepreneurs, a crucible for conversations that change futures. Coen Jonker, Tjaart van der Walt and Nate Clarke were in the US on a fundraising trip that, quite conveniently, overlapped with the Endeavor gala where Vélez was slated as the guest of honour.

At a pre-gala 'fireside chat' with Vélez, Clarke introduced himself as a founder of GoTyme in the Philippines, and he posed a question to Vélez. Clarke coyly reports that he doesn't remember the question he posed, but Vélez's response included a casual note that he had heard of the African outfit making waves in Southeast Asia. Then the Endeavor president, Adrian Garcia-Aranyos, helped make a connection between the two, suggesting they should talk – after all, they were rivals in strategy, if not geography. They spoke for five minutes, enough to spark curiosity, not enough to form plans.

Playing it cool

The next morning brought a moment of symmetry – the Tyme and Nubank teams found themselves in the same elevator. A brief exchange, polite and professional. There was some doubt among the Tyme delegation as to whether they were even recognised. Jonker, ever eager, wanted to seize the opportunity being presented to them with both hands – his father's words *carpe diem* echoing in his mind. Van der Walt advised restraint. If a partnership was to be built, it had to be peer-to-peer, not pitched with any hint of desperation.

Later that night, over pints in a dimly lit Irish bar, Clarke and Jonker wondered aloud: what if Nubank invested in Tyme? Not just admiration, but alignment.

Three months passed. Then Jonker made the call. Informal. Measured. Tyme had just kicked off its Series D capital raise. Would Nubank be interest in joining the round? The timing was perfect. Vélez and Junqueira were heading to South Africa and Southeast Asia to meet banks and exchange notes with others in the industry. One of those meetings would prove pivotal.

The Tyme for talks

In Cape Town, the conversation got serious. Was Tyme for sale? Absolutely not, Jonker replied. But they welcomed strategic investment. Days later they met in Shenzhen, which was on Nubank's itinerary and where Clarke and Aaron Foo also attended a Tencent investee conference. Foo was dubbed 'Harvard Aaron', thanks to his strong academic credentials and next-level thinking. The Chinese firm had taken stakes in more than 30 neobanks, which included both Nubank and Tyme. It also so happened that Nubank would be in Manila the following week. Vélez offered Clarke and Foo a ride on his Gulfstream private jet, which helped facilitate the whistle-stop tour. The jet pitch was memorable. Onboard, Clarke connected his laptop to the in-flight screen and presented the Tyme story. It was a rare moment of undivided attention from one of the most respected teams in global fintech. Foo recalls how impressed he was by Nubank's depth: 'They asked questions with probing detail. They knew all the pain points, from tech stack to growth strategy.'

However, while serendipitous, this first presentation had not gone well. Junqueira had noted that TymeBank's net promoter score in South Africa lagged behind another digital bank, Discovery Bank. Clarke offered explanations about the difference in the markets served by TymeBank and Discovery Bank, including differences in digital engagement, and the characteristics and behaviour of the two bank's clients. That was not enough to make the case. But when the Nubank team visited GoTyme in the

Philippines, their doubts and reservations were quickly reversed. GoTyme's younger customer base, digital affinity and leaner structure delivered a customer experience that changed minds – and specifically the minds of the Nubank team.

Initially sceptical of Tyme's partnership model, Nubank worried about losing control over customer outcomes. But what they saw in Manila, and later in Vietnam, shifted their view. Tyme was obsessive about governance and fanatical about service. That fanaticism tipped the balance. In reflecting on the merits of the investment that reinforced the case for Nubank, CFO Guilherme Lago explains that Nubank had developed a clear framework for assessing attractive markets: sufficient population scale, deep mobile penetration, progressive regulators, openness to foreign capital and under-penetrated or mispriced credit. 'When we applied that lens,' he says, 'countries like South Africa, the Philippines and Indonesia stood out. Tyme was already in all of them. It was only a matter of time before we found each other.'

Lago also notes that beyond Tyme's presence in the right markets, several elements stood out to Nubank. They were intrigued by Tyme's phygital business model – blending digital reach with physical access points – and impressed by the depth of the management team's knowledge, experience and execution capability. Just as important, he emphasises, was the team's intellectual humility: their openness to feedback, willingness to engage on tough questions and ability to be challenged without defensiveness. Finally, Tyme's cultural intelligence in markets where Nubank had little on-the-ground experience was seen as a strategic asset.

Negotiating with unicorns

But alignment came with tension. Nubank's initial term sheet included an aggressive clause: the right to acquire more shares at a later stage at the same valuation. Jonker was clear: this was not on the table. Negotiations stretched over weeks – and weekends. Foo describes Lago as pleasant but unyielding. With persistence, Lago and Foo reached what felt like consensus. However, when documents came back from Lago, Foo says many of the concessions had been qualified, and the deal almost fell apart. Notwithstanding the gaps and places where they were missing each other, both sides wanted to find each other – they wanted a deal. Drafting full contracts began in mid-August. By October, with a lot of debate and deliberation, the deal still wasn't done. Tyme had hoped to announce the investment at Singapore's prestigious FinTech Festival in November, but timelines slipped. Then Jonker stepped in personally and his years of corporate deal-making and some of the lessons learnt in 217 investor calls in the darkest days of Covid bore fruit.

In December 2024, the deal closed. Nubank took a 10% stake in Tyme. The valuation: US$1.5 billion. Tyme had joined the unicorn club. 'We had finally been knighted in the global court of fintech,' Jonker said. 'This puts us in a small club of banks to be watched.'

The deal brought more than capital. It brought perspective, networks and strategic depth.

From an elevator in New York to hitching a ride in a private jet over the South China Sea, Tyme had moved from being a fan of Nubank to becoming its peer – and partner. Tyme had moved from the edge of the industry to its centre.

The uncertainty of prediction, it turns out, is not a limitation. It is an invitation. To dream, to bet, to build.

Chapter 15

Here's to the Crazy Ones

Live in the future, then build what's missing.
— Paul Graham

Dreaming with discipline

Over a coffee at the airport on our return from two weeks in Manila, Ho Chi Minh and Singapore, we deliberated: What if we're writing this book too early? What if we've drunk the Kool-Aid? Had we been immersed for so long that we had come down with mild Stockholm syndrome? Most businesses fail – what makes Tyme an exception?

We reflected on a question that we had posed to Tuan Bui. 'Do you sometimes think Coen is mad?' His response mirrored our own: 'Yeah, sometimes.' But every mould-smashing success that ever was or ever will be is driven by someone quite mad. Like the opening to Apple's iconic 1997 advert: 'Here's to the crazy ones …'

One last time, we turn to the enigmatic Madame Clicquot – surely crazy in her own way. In a letter to a grandchild, she wrote, 'The world is in perpetual motion, and we must invent the things of tomorrow. One must go before others, be determined and exacting, and let your intelligence direct your life. Act with audacity.'

Craziness alone (or is audacity the word?) is no help to anyone. It is where crazy meets purpose that things like iPods and aeroplanes come about. That balance is one we wish we could have articulated in this book.

Instead, we learnt that it is something beyond articulation. All we can do is to understand it as best as we can and embrace it intelligently.

Crazy ideas are also no help if they come with dreams and no action. Coen Jonker and Tjaart van der Walt are dreamers. There is no doubt about it. But not the idle sort. 'All men dream,' wrote T.E. Lawrence, 'but not equally. Those who dream by night in the dusty recesses of their minds wake in the day to find that it was vanity: but the dreamers of the day are dangerous men, for they may act on their dreams with open eyes, to make them possible.'[1] Jonker and Van der Walt dream all day and all night.

To understand these dreams, we have asked many questions of other people. Now we were asking more of ourselves. What if the signals we have read as strengths – Tyme's capital-light model, its deep partnerships and its ability to scale across country borders without branches – turn out to be vulnerabilities? What if the very markets that offer the greatest opportunity for financial inclusion also prove the most unforgiving to a business trying to rewrite the rules? After all, history is littered with the wreckages of high-potential ventures undone by regulatory shifts, economic downturns or big changes in consumer behaviour. Even among digital-first financial firms, success is rare, and resilience is tested in ways that do not appear in spreadsheets or pitch decks.

During this airport coffee conversation, we were reminded of *Top ICT Companies in South Africa*, a book produced by the Corporate Research Foundation at the turn of the century.[2] It was written by an international consortium of in-the-know infotech and financial journalists, academics, publishers and leading industry analysts. In writing that book, they had set out to assess the prospects of what were then considered the most promising information technology businesses in South Africa. The list ranged from niche fintech firms, such as like Abraxas Technologies, DexData and Zaptronix, to established global players like Hewlett-Packard, Oracle and SAP. While a fascinating read at the time, the book now serves as a cautionary tale for anyone attempting to forecast the future.

Of the 61 companies covered, 46 have failed or disappeared (75%), four were acquired (7%) and just 11 remain operational (18%). Perhaps even more striking is that only one company listed in the infotech cluster of the Johannesburg Stock Exchange today receives mention in the book, while the most successful South African tech investment of the past 25 years – Naspers, through its stake in Chinese giant Tencent – is conspicuously absent from the list.

Most digital banks will fail. This game is capital-intensive, tightly regulated, operationally unforgiving and demands scale at speed. A 2024 UBS Investment Bank study of over 50 digital banks across Asia drives the point home.[3] Most are losing money. In fact, among the digital banks launched in ASEAN over the past five years, less than 10% are profitable. Only a handful – like Korea's KakaoBank or China's MYbank – have reached sustainability. Many are stuck in what analysts now call a scale trap: spending heavily on acquisition and product build, without achieving the customer depth or operating leverage to turn a profit.

Nubank's Guilherme Lago observes that some of the biggest risks facing Tyme lie outside the company's control – chief among them, how markets evolve in response to rising financial inclusion, real-time payments and accelerating digital penetration. These forces are reshaping the landscape and demand that firms move ever faster. But not all risks are external. Within Tyme's control, the challenge lies in responding swiftly to change, while preserving the integrity of systems and customer trust. As Lago puts it, unlike other corners of fintech where it is acceptable to 'move fast and break things', in banking, the bar is higher: you have to move fast and break nothing. On that front, he is deeply complimentary of Tyme's risk infrastructure and system design, comparing it favourably to Nubank's own, which is widely regarded as best-in-class, despite operating with just one-twentieth the headcount of incumbent banks. In Lago's words, both firms are setting a new gold standard for how digital banks manage credit and market risk.

UBS identifies three characteristics that separate winners from the rest. The most successful digital banks excel in three areas: ecosystem leverage, cost efficiency and cross-sell economics. First, the most successful players are embedded in much larger digital ecosystems. WeBank and MYbank, backed by Tencent and Alibaba respectively, launched with access to hundreds of millions of users. Platforms like Grab, SEA and GoTo, which span e-commerce, ride-hailing, payments and credit, effectively convert digital traffic into banking scale. Second, the winners run lean. Leading digital banks like KakaoBank operate with expense-to-asset ratios between 0.5% and 2.5%. By contrast, UBS estimates that most ASEAN digital banks are operating at ratios of 6.5% to 16%. These levels are unsustainable without rapid growth or significant cross-selling. Third, profitability increasingly depends on generating non-interest income through cross-selling insurance, investment products and payments, and through lending. Banks that merely acquire depositors are not breaking even. Instead, the most successful digital banks are those that convert users into multi-product customers.

Against this harsh benchmark, Tyme shows quiet strength. It does not dominate headlines like Grab, GCash, Maya or SeaBank, and it does not benefit from China-scale ecosystems or state backing. But it does possess the core DNA that UBS calls out as critical.

Tyme's customer acquisition cost is among the lowest globally – a result of its hybrid kiosk model, partnerships with major retailers and contextualised onboarding journeys. It runs on a single shared platform (TymeX), giving it embedded operating leverage as it scales across markets. And it is already building multi-product relationships – from deposits to buy now, pay later (BNPL), to merchant lending – designed to drive deeper unit economics.

Jesse Lucas, GoTyme's chief consumer credit and data analytics officer, applies this thinking to help unleash the power of credit. 'People in the Philippines live day to day. Banks don't lend and interest rates are very high. Our ambition is to use data to build credit that is accessible and affordable. Launching our first BNPL product is evidence of what we can do. The Philippines is data-poor, and this product is a chance to gather high-quality credit data. Through this, we will release more credit as experience grows.'

Perhaps most important, Tyme's business model was forged in hard places, through some of the most unexpected challenges to hit the business world in the last century. It was not built with subsidies or softened by policy support. It grew out of a need to serve financially excluded populations in South Africa, the Philippines and now Indonesia. That has made the company fiercely focused on operational discipline, customer relevance and capital efficiency.

Still, in writing a book about a business in motion – and not a memoir – we accept the risk we have taken on: the outcome of many of the aspects we have written about won't be known for some time; others will be known by the time this book is in print. Either way, there are no guarantees of long-term success or failure – for us in our writing, or for Tyme as a business. Should we be doing this?

We resolved that the risk is a good one to take. And, regardless of what the future holds, telling the Tyme story is worthwhile in and of itself. The exploration is full of lessons. The business is in the middle of fantastic industrial change, which has the potential to alter the lives of millions of people, tens of millions, and perhaps even a hundred million. Jonker is confident that in the next ten years, the biggest and most profitable retail banks in the world will be digital. We share this view. Jonker enthuses further that Tyme will rank among the global giants.

Some reckon that is hubristic. Sim Tshabalala, the chief executive officer of banking giant Standard Bank, belongs to the less charitable group. He thinks the valuation of the US$1.5 billion that Nubank and others paid in the recent Series D capital raise is nonsensical, that established banks have caught up to the lead that Tyme and others once had, and that even if the incumbents haven't yet caught up, the challengers, in the main, are yet to make profit, and most never will – making these speculative adventures, at best. Nubank's Lago pushes back on this view: 'Traditional banks are not asleep at the wheel,' he notes. 'Some, like HSBC, Standard Chartered and Citibank, have responded impressively – but they're the exception, not the rule.'

As is the norm with Tyme, there are worthy opposing views. 'Nubank's due diligence was the most intense diligence process I have experienced,' says Tyme's Quynh Ngo, speaking from an extensive career with multi-bank, multi-country experience. Nubank's valuation was no stab in the dark.

Culture feeds strategy

Why do we think Tyme has a real shot at global success when we know the odds are stacked against it? Our time close to the business has revealed a rare trait with strong predictive powers of success. Anyone can build a good strategy. Something else makes that work.

Management consultant Peter Drucker famously quipped: 'Culture eats strategy for breakfast.' In our collective experience, having worked in a number of businesses – including our own firms – across industries and with 70 cumulative years of work experience, we agree. But, at the risk of going up against the legendary Drucker, perhaps his observation is incomplete.

What if culture feeds breakfast to strategy? We make this observation because the culture that permeates Tyme is unmistakable, unshakable and authentic, and that feeds purpose, Sisyphean determination and a willingness to roll the rock differently, or roll a different rock, or perhaps even roll the rock up a different hill, sometimes a hill nobody else thought of. In a word, agility. And this makes for a powerful cultural compact.

The problem with culture is that it is hard to define. But, as US Supreme Court Justice Potter Stewart famously remarked in the 1964 case *Jacobellis v. Ohio*, when struggling to define pornography, 'I know it when I see it.' The same holds true for organisational culture – it often defies rigid definition, yet its presence (or absence) is unmistakable. It is the invisible force that shapes behaviours, decisions and the very essence of a company.

At Tyme, culture is not just a backdrop. It is an active, driving force that feeds a shared purpose, fuels determination and cultivates agility – which is why a series of failed corporate marriages did not break the team; it bound them tighter in their pursuit. Tyme's culture enables the team.

Like many corporations, Tyme has words, boards and mission statements posted around its offices in all locations. But in the Philippines, a digital board with scrolling posters landed some big points that stand out in Tyme's purpose, belief, lived experience and ambition.

A poster in the Manila office punts: 'We want to build the biggest retail bank in the country by 2028.' And some words have been crossed out in permanent marker and written over by hand, so that the ambition re-reads: 'We will build the most loved retail bank in the country by 2028.'

Leadership happens through context, not control – people aren't micromanaged; they are trusted to figure things out. This came up time and again in conversations throughout the business.

Van der Walt captures the Tyme approach. 'In firms with inspirational leadership, power comes from the endorsement of the leaders by their subordinates. They trust the leader's intent and ability. In transactional organisations, power comes from the top.'

Tyme does not see itself as a niche play or moderate success; the ambition is to win at scale. It is worth citing more: 'We encourage bold decisions, many of which will fail. We embrace, learn from and even go as far as celebrating those failures. We must be great; good is not good enough. Reimagining banking is not just about new products and innovations; it is about doing the basics better than anyone else. We believe simplicity is synonymous with beauty. Less is more.' And this thinking is pervasive – and contagious.

Simplicity shines through in a set of design principles that Van der Walt listed for us early on:

- No employees handle cash.
- No paper.
- No credit committee – this is done by straight-through processing.
- No bricks and mortar.
- Account opening in under five minutes.

It is also clear that this is a business that is building solutions for customers – not because of customers. And a business that sees a fundamental goodness in people and their intent. 'We are huge fans of our customers and colleagues. We cheer them along their path to success. We hold each other to the highest standards of integrity, respect and honesty; we courageously hold people to account if they fall short. We believe the best idea should always prevail, not the view of the most senior person. We expect each other to speak out when something isn't right; silent disagreement is not tolerated. We admit mistakes – to each other and to our customers. We always assume positive intent, from our customers and each other.'

A cynical perspective finds this hard to accept – the 'veneer theory' suggests that civilisation is a fragile shell covering human savagery, and that, left to our own devices, we behave like Jack Merridew and his 'hunters' in *Lord of the Flies*.[4] Jonker rejects this view, and we spent time instead discussing Rutger Bregman's *Humankind: A Hopeful History*.[5]

Bregman dismantles the idea that people default to selfishness. He points to real-life cases, like a group of Tongan boys shipwrecked in 1965. Unlike the fictional schoolboys William Golding portrayed on an unnamed island, this real-life group survived for over a year by cooperating.

Studies of disaster responses – from plane crashes to hurricanes – consistently show that panic and chaos are the exception, not the rule. Survivors help each other, often at great personal risk. This aligns with David Hume's argument that 'the sentiments of benevolence and humanity, however feeble, are present in some degree' in all people.[6] Hume recognised that kindness and goodness are not anomalies – they are intrinsic to human nature. In our discussion, Jonker nodded at this point. His conviction that positive intent is not naive but a strategic advantage, comes not from blind optimism but from a belief – supported by history, philosophy and behavioural science – that people, given the chance, will usually do the right thing.

In Vietnam, TymeX has been ranked among the best places to work. More clues come from the digital posters: 'We hire people full of questions, not answers. We attract people who aren't scared to get their hands dirty and run towards, not away from, the fires. We think as owners, not renters of the business. We invest and spend as if the money is our own.' And perhaps this one is written by Jonker because it certainly resonates: 'We are a good home for those with scars and unfinished business. We like people who have lost battles but have the hunger to fight again.'

And the drumroll? 'We are creators.' And the ambition on the giant wall poster in the Manila office sets out the targets for 2028: a net promoter score of 80 (the numbers 70, and then 72 had been crossed out by hand); SAVii's net operating income to reach 1.1 billion pesos; to be the top bank in monthly app active users, with 2.2 million users; and to be the country's top employer. These aren't words – they are explicit targets underpinned by shared vision, collective belief and common purpose.

One sentiment from Raymund Villanueva resonates. 'Drop the word digital and inject the word human,' he suggests. 'This is what will make us the most beautiful bank in the Philippines.'

During our breakfast in Cape Town late in 2024, Jonker shared a story that explains this. He recalls a story told by Ben Zander, the renowned musical director of the Boston Philharmonic Orchestra and the Boston Philharmonic Youth Orchestra.

As he remembers it, the youth orchestra had been working on Vivaldi's 'Four Seasons'. As the rehearsal was about to start one day, the lead violinist approached Zander, clearly distressed. He put his arms around Zander, weeping. His heart had been broken – his relationship of the past year, his first and only love, had come to an end. Zander pulled the youth close to comfort him and smiled. Now he would be able to play the second movement of 'Winter' with understanding. As much as the heartbreak was deeply hurtful and sad, it would give the young lead violinist true understanding of what a broken heart really felt like. When people truly understand, they produce the best work, Jonker said. Tyme's ambassadors are all Tyme bank account holders; Lance Gokongwei is a Tyme bank account holder. They get it. Beyond understanding, they know.

Next, our breakfast conversation meandered to *The Art of Possibility: Transforming Professional and Personal Life*, the book Ben Zander co-wrote with Rosamund Stone Zander.[7] A masterful blend of leadership philosophy, personal development and creative thinking, the book distils lessons from music, psychology and business to inspire new ways of seeing the world. As a conductor, Zander realised that his real power wasn't in wielding authority but in creating the conditions for others to shine. His measure of success became simple: were the eyes around him shining?

That idea struck a chord. We had both seen this at Tyme. It is impossible to miss – peoples' eyes do shine. His response was immediate, almost instinctive: '*I love that.*' In that moment, we saw something rare – a leader who was not just building a business but drawing profound fulfilment from the engagement and energy of his team. The work was not just about execution or scale; it was about possibility, purpose and people. And you could see it, quite literally, in their eyes.

Wall Street or bust? SoFi, Nubank and the Tyme test

Listing is often treated like a pinnacle. Founders pop Champagne and purchase yachts. Initial public offering (IPO) is the ultimate 'We've arrived!' Really, it is a wonderful, nervy and fleeting moment. Listing your business comes with the challenge of turning all that money you raised into lots more money! At times, it arrives as the ultimate case of 'be careful what you wish for, you just might get it'. Now you must execute on the growth strategy you have sold.

Case studies of digital-first financial services firms listing in the US are few and recent. However, in helping us pull this story together, there are precedents to learn from.

SoFi Technologies listed on the Nasdaq at the start of June 2021. The fintech emerged out of Stanford's Graduate School of Business in 2011 as a pioneering peer-to-peer student loan refinancing project, wielding data science as its secret sauce to lower costs. SoFi (short for Social Finance) received approval as a national bank in the US in January of 2022 and now offers everything from retail banking and personal loans to insurance and travel.[8]

Any takeaways from their stock performance should be taken in the light of the milieu. The IPO was amid the Covid era. A poor opening year turned into two flat years, followed by a minor lift since October 2024. In sum, those who bought on day one and held are down about 5%.

SoFi reached 1 million customers ('members' in their lingo) in January of 2020. By the end of September 2024, they reported ten times growth: over 10 million customers. Collectively, these clients had earned over US$1 billion in interest on savings, paid down US$33 billion in credit-card debt and borrowed US$117 billion.[9]

PART IV: THE SECOND TYME

The many trials of Tyme documented throughout this book should have primed us for this. Digital banking is not for wimps – be it management teams or investors. And it is certainly not for the impatient. As much as a kiosk or website can speed up individual processes, this is an emerging business model with plenty to learn.

SoFi exhibits some parallels with Tyme. CEO Anthony Noto brings energy, vision and vast experience. An engineer with an MBA, he was an army ranger for a spell, served two periods with Goldman Sachs and spent nearly three years as CFO of the National Football League before joining Twitter (as X then was) for several C-suite roles just ahead of joining SoFi in 2018.

Few would disagree with *Wharton Magazine*'s take that 'Noto has made a career of thinking big'. Noto offers an analogy that hints at the nature of running a digital bank: 'The light bulb is one of the greatest innovations in the world. What got the light bulb invented wasn't the idea. It was the thousands of iterations of the different filament, of different voltages, of different currents. The light bulb is still being improved today because of iteration.'[10]

He goes on, 'One of our core values at SoFi is to iterate, learn, iterate, learn. If you don't have a culture of iterating and learning, you'll never drive innovation. You'll just have a bunch of ideas that fail.'

On his decision to join SoFi at the helm, Noto again sounds like he would fit right in at Tyme. 'I wanted to be a CEO of a company at some point, but it wasn't the right time. The more I thought about SoFi, I saw it as a chance to do something that no one had ever done in financial services – what Amazon had done in retail and what Netflix had done in entertainment, which was to completely disrupt the industry and become the incumbent leader as the winner that takes most.'

Perhaps an even better trailblazer to learn from is Nubank – now a major investor in Tyme. The neobank with roots in Brazil listed on the New York Stock Exchange well under a decade after its founding in 2013. The digital-first bank's secret sauce was dealing with stifling bureaucracy and high fees in Brazil's banking system, offering individual customers simple, online solutions.

This speaks to South Africa, where established banks are still heavily reliant on fee-paying customers.

Nubank founder David Vélez's 2023 reflection on the company's first decade offers shades of the Tyme attitude: 'Exactly ten years ago, a Brazilian, an American and a Colombian were able to finally incorporate their start-up with an odd choice of name: Nubank, or "banco nu".[11] The name, and the chosen purple colour, were unorthodox decisions for a new bank in the conservative financial services space. But the team felt that there was an opportunity to challenge conventional wisdom and create a new institution that was consumer-obsessed, simple and transparent, and that "provided oxygen" to an industry badly needing it.

'The experts cautioned that the enterprise was doomed, as it was impossible to build a new, digital bank. But the team listened and concluded that smartphones were a complete change of paradigm, and that consumers were ready for new alternatives. With *frio na barriga* [butterflies in the tummy], the team pitched to their potential investors, going from 12 customers in 2013 to 1 million by 2019 – most investors declined.'

Vélez could back up the bravado. In a decade, they had acquired 80 million customers in Latin America. One in two Brazilians with smartphones were Nubank customers.

He concluded, 'We have saved 248 million hours for our customers and over US$8 billion in fees that have remained in our customers' pockets. And we have brought positive competition to an industry that was too concentrated: banking concentration in Brazil has gone from 70% in 2014 to 58% at the end of 2022.' Not bad for a precocious ten-year-old born in a small house in São Paulo.

The world has noticed. In 2025, Nubank was ranked third on Fast Company's The World's 50 Most Innovative Companies and took top spot in the category for Finance and Personal Finance. They now boast 114 million customers across Brazil, Mexico and Colombia, and posted 2024 revenues of US$11.5 billion, with a return on equity of 28%. Globally, banks achieved a return on equity of 12.3% in 2024.

PART IV: THE SECOND TYME

Digital premium or emerging market discount?
A keystone trait that Nubank shares with Tyme, but not with SoFi, is its emerging market status. Like Tyme, Nubank has roots in the developing world. Despite listing amid the bright lights of New York City, this attracts a risk profile that Californian-headquartered SoFi does not.

Through the lens of 'emerging market stock', companies like Nubank and Tyme are associated with several headwinds, regardless of the nature of their operations. Most importantly, investors apply a risk premium. Political environments in South America, Africa and emerging Asia are viewed as more unstable than developed markets. Institutions are not as well formed, and progress is less predictable. Currencies are more volatile. Corporate governance and transparency are also lumped in as typical weaknesses for emerging market shares. Of course, the quality of reporting standards and oversight vary among developing countries. But investors demand a premium to take on exposure outside of the advanced, established markets, where the biggest analysts are watching shares like hawks.

All of those barriers are surmountable. For one thing, the case can be made that the West has lost some of its stability premium in recent years. Trade wars by tweet are a notable example of novel volatility among advanced economies. We can add heightened risk of conflict, too. Established two-party electoral environments are also under pressure.

Emerging markets have tailwinds of their own, too. Stable Europe certainly does not offer the growth prospects on offer in parts of the developing world. Africa alone is home to roughly half of the planet's fastest-growing economies.[12] The IMF reckons advanced economies grew just 1.7% in 2024, compared to a global average of 3.2%, and an emerging market and developing economies average of 4.2%.[13]

To be sure, China's rampant growth has eased back from its breakneck speed of recent years, frequently in double digits. Just under 5% is still highly enviable for most nations. India is charting along handsomely with a predicted 6.5% per year for the next couple of years. In Africa, superstar GDP growers include Senegal (9.3%), Libya (13.7%) and Ethiopia (6.5%)

– and the two fastest-growing economies in the world over the last 25 years are Ethiopia and Rwanda, not China and India.

The geography hack: Going global with MultiX

Tyme's strategy has one facet that leaps off the page as an antidote to emerging market share pricing. If Tyme can get MultiX right, they will leave outdated notions like geography in their dust. A truly online bank with the capacity to cross borders fast and at low cost is not an emerging market bank. It is also not a developed market bank. If headquartered in Singapore and listed on a major exchange, it is a truly global bank. It can follow demand wherever it may be. That turns a risk premium on its head.

Nubank's experience offers a lesson, too. While much of the emerging market aura is outside the control of any individual business, there is one sure-fire way to escape it: rise above it. If your vision, leadership, product and performance are good enough, investors will respond. A booming customer base, rising profits, compelling narrative and unquestionable commitment to ethics, innovation and impact will go a long way to fuelling escape velocity from any regional risk lens.

We reckon Tyme has shown the grit needed to win as a digital bank. It feels like it is in their DNA. In Tjaart van der Walt's case, it is. Van der Walt's father built the leading food brand Nola mayonnaise against all odds, dethroning the entrenched giant Crosse & Blackwell, despite being told there was no room for another player. His maternal grandfather, Etienne Rousseau, founded Sasol in 1950, further establishing the belief that exceptional businesses can be built from South Africa. His forebears would be unsurprised by his approach to building Tyme: 'We can build and compete with the best in the world, even born in a small market.'

Tyme's financial performance reflects the spoils of grit. At last reporting, Tyme had achieved profit in South Africa and was approaching break-even in the Philippines. The business model suggests that Tyme has the basis for top-line growth of 50% per annum over the next five years, which would create a business seven-and-a-half times its current size, with an expected return on equity of 40% per annum, more than triple the global average for banks.

A successful floating on a major exchange will demand one addition to this. While building to their listing, Tyme needs to go from a largely unknown entity to an attractive risk-return proposition in order to attract America's institutional investors. This means telling a compelling story to the right audiences. In the run-up to a listing, you need to have locked in serious names for large commitments to equity. The rest follow on IPO day.

This Tyme is different

We are not sure where the tale of Tyme lands up – a listing on a major exchange in 2028, absorbed into the greater Nubank group as a shining Asian and African beacon, a business filled with ambition but caught in crosswinds, or a shattered dream? It is impossible to know. Is the vision of a 100-million-customer, multi-country digital bank within reach? Are the structural and regulatory challenges too significant to overcome, or has Tyme demonstrated a model that can be replicated and scaled?

Tyme's approach to partnerships, a core strategy that Tjaart van der Walt learnt at the family dinner table that 'business does not have to be a zero-sum game', opens a world of opportunity for the group. Just hours before this book was sent to the printers, Paul Hanratty, the CEO of Africa's biggest insurance company, Sanlam, which has a presence in 30 countries on the continent, revealed that Sanlam and Tyme would form a retail credit joint venture focused on unsecured personal loans with an embedded credit life offering. The deal should come as no surprise. Sanlam has a 25% stake in African Rainbow Capital Financial Services Investments (ARC FSI). While insurance rival Old Mutual had spent a reported R2.8 billion building a bank from scratch with a goal of breaking even in 2028, and retailer Shoprite revealed it was considering broadening its financial services, Sanlam has an oven-ready offering to put to the market.

As one learns in *The Gap in the Curtain* by John Buchan, 'Success depends on seeing just a little more into the future than other people.'[14] If we have achieved our ambition with this book, readers have a better chance of seeing just a little further into the future of digital banking than the rest.

Here is what we do know. Tyme has already achieved incredible things that many thought impossible. It has a culture that will embrace its lofty ambitions. Tyme is adept at appreciating best practice, and then intelligently breaking loose from it. And in a world where partnership is key, Tyme's reputation will make future partnerships easier and easier.

If you ask us, this Tyme is different.

Notes

Preface: This Ain't No Fairy Tale

1. P. Knight, *Shoe Dog: A Memoir by the Creator of Nike* (New York: Scribner, 2016).
2. H. Schultz with D. Jones Yang, *Pour Your Heart into It: How Starbucks Built a Company One Cup at a Time* (New York: Hyperion, 1997).
3. R. Branson, *Losing My Virginity: How I Survived, Had Fun, and Made a Fortune Doing Business My Way* (New York: Crown Business, 1998).
4. P. Ormerod, *Why Most Things Fail: Evolution, Extinction and Economics* (London: Faber & Faber, 2005).

Chapter 2: The Wrong Plus-One

1. H. de Soto, *The Mystery of Capital: Why Capitalism Triumphs in the West and Fails Everywhere Else* (New York: Basic Books, 2000).
2. South African Reserve Bank, *Annual Report*, 2007/08, https://www.gov.za/sites/default/files/gcis_document/201409/sa-reserve-bankannualreport20072008.pdf.
3. Bankable Frontier Associates, 'The Mzansi Bank Account Initiative in South Africa: Final Report', 2009, https://finmark.org.za/system/documents/files/000/000/316/original/MsanziBankAccInitiativeSA_2009.pdf?1614593520.

Chapter 3: From Branches to Backends

1. 'Nu Holdings Ltd. Reports Third Quarter 2024 Financial Results', 13 November 2024, https://rb.gy/ua3bld.
2. World Bank, 'The Global Findex Database 2021: Financial Inclusion, Digital Payments, and Resilience in the Age of COVID-19', 2021, www.worldbank.org/en/publication/globalfindex.
3. Federal Reserve Bank of St. Louis, FRED Database, https://fred.stlouisfed.org.
4. P. Ghemawat, *World 3.0: Global Prosperity and How to Achieve It* (Brighton, MA: Harvard Business Review Press, 2011).
5. S.A. Altman and C.R. Bastian, *DHL Global Connectedness Report 2024*, DOI: 10.58153/7jt4h-p0738.

NOTES

6 G. Parker, M. van Alstyne and S.P. Choudary, *Platform Revolution: How Networked Markets Are Transforming the Economy and How to Make Them Work for You* (New York: W.W. Norton & Company, 2016); M.A. Cusumano, A. Gawer and D.B. Yoffie, *The Business of Platforms: Strategy in the Age of Digital Competition, Innovation, and Power* (New York: Harper Business, 2019); A. Tiwana, *Platform Ecosystems: Aligning Architecture, Governance, and Strategy* (Burlington, MA: Morgan Kaufmann, 2014); J-C. Rochet and J. Tirole, 'Platform Competition in Two-Sided Markets', *Journal of the European Economic Association* 1(4), 2003: 990–1029; A. Hagiu and J. Wright, 'Multi-Sided Platforms', *International Journal of Industrial Organization* 43, 2015: 162–174.

7 World Bank, *World Development Report 2019: The Changing Nature of Work* (Washington, DC: World Bank, 2019), DOI:10.1596/978-1-4648-1328-3.

8 Notably, while models that ramp up in this fashion often lead to the celebration of founders and firms, it is the foundation of technology that scales and connects that is the real celebration: John Kay's flying shuttle (1733); James Watt's significant improvements to the steam engine (1769); Samuel Morse's telegraph (1837); Ada Lovelace's computer algorithm (1840s); Alexander Graham Bell's telephone (1876); Hedy Lamarr's frequency-hopping spread spectrum (1940s); or Tim Berners-Lee's World Wide Web. Never diminishing the contributions of the brilliant minds who commercialise these innovations, it is the technology that provides the platform and foundation for scaling. To drive true transformation, labs and corporations need accelerants, and the most powerful accelerant is globalisation. There were 20,000 miles of railways in the world when the American Civil War ended in 1865. There were 300,000 miles in 1914. There are a million miles of rail worldwide today. See J.B. DeLong, *Slouching towards Utopia: An Economic History of the Twentieth Century* (New York: Basic Books, 2022).

9 C. Sidar, 'Suddenly AI: The Fastest Adopted Business Technology in History', Forbes, 2023, https://www.forbes.com/councils/forbestechcouncil/2023/04/05/suddenly-ai-the-fastest-adopted-business-technology-in-history/.

10 H. Dediu, 'Seeing What's Next', Asymco, 18 November 2013, www.asymco.com/2013/11/18/seeing-whats-next-2/; H. Dediu, 'The Frontiers of Platform Adoption', Asymco, 2022, https://www.asymco.com/2011/07/16/the-frontiers-of-platform-adoption/

11 RevenueCat, 'The State of Subscription Apps 2025', 24 January 2025, https://www.revenuecat.com/state-of-subscription-apps-2025/.

12 A. McKay (director), *Talladega Nights: The Ballad of Ricky Bobby*, 2006 [film].

13 David Vélez quoted by D. Leone, 'Nubank IPO: Only the Beginning', *Sequoia*, 9 December 2021, www.sequoiacap.com/article/nubank-ipo-only-the-beginning/. The statement is mistakenly attributed to Mahatma Gandhi; the origin of the statement traces to Nicholas Klein, a trade union activist, who said something similar in a 1918 speech, saying, 'First they ignore you. Then they ridicule you. And then they attack you and want to burn you. And then they build monuments to you.'

Chapter 4: Hidden in Plain Sight

1 L. Guiso, P. Sapienza and L. Zingales, 'Trusting the Stock Market', *The Journal of Finance* 63(6), 2008: 2557–2600, https://doi.org/10.1111/j.1540-6261.2008.01408.x.

2 N. Lioudis, 'The Collapse of Lehman Brothers: A Case Study', Investopedia, 26 November 2019, https://www.vbsoexpertise.com.br/wp-content/uploads/2020/09/AULA-03-The-Collapse-of-Lehman-Brothers_-A-Case-Study.pdf.

3 M. Fenwick and E.P.M. Vermeulen, 'Technology and Corporate Governance: Blockchain, Crypto, and Artificial Intelligence'. Working Paper No. 2018-7, http://dx.doi.org/10.2139/ssrn.3263222.

4 C.K. Prahalad, *The Fortune at the Bottom of the Pyramid: Eradicating Poverty through Profits*, revised edition (Philadelphia, PA: Wharton School Press, 2010).

5 J. Clift, 'Hearing the Dogs Bark', *Finance & Development* 40(4), 2003: 8–12.

6 We actively replace the original term 'poor' in the quote with 'excluded'.

7 Clift, 'Hearing the Dogs Bark': 8–12.

8 R. Levine, 'Financial Development and Economic Growth: Views and Agenda', *Journal of Economic Literature* 35(2), 1997: 688–726.

9 A.D. Saville and I. Macleod, *Saving, Investment and Socio-Economic Transformation: Investec-GIBS Savings Index*, 3rd edition (Johannesburg: Investec, 2019).

10 A. Saville, I. Macleod and T. Onaji-Benson, *Platforms of Prosperity: The Africa Edition* (Pretoria: Gordon Institute of Business Science, 2021).

11 Centre for Finance, Technology and Entrepreneurship, 'The World's Top 5 Unbanked Countries Have More Than 60% of Their Population without Bank Accounts', *CFTE*, 13 June 2023, https://blog.cfte.education/the-worlds-top-5-unbanked-countries-have-more-than-60-of-their-population-without-bank-accounts/#:~:text=A%20recent%20study%20by%20the,60%25%20of%20their%20population%20unbanked.

12 'Financial Inclusion in Sub-Saharan Africa: Overview', World Bank, 17 April 2024, https://www.worldbank.org/en/publication/globalfindex/brief/financial-inclusion-in-sub-saharan-africa-overview.

13 M. Yunus, *Banker to the Poor: Micro-Lending and the Battle against World Poverty* (New York: PublicAffairs, 2003); E. Rhyne, 'The Yin and Yang of Microfinance: Reaching the Poor and Sustainability', *MicroBanking Bulletin*, July 1988, https://www.microfinancelessons.com/files/media_subdomain/resources/rhyne_yingyang.pdf.

14 'Impact 2023: Global Goals, Local Change', *Grameen Foundation*, 2023, https://grameenfoundation.org/documents/Grameen-Foundation-Impact-Brief-2023.pdf.

15 S.R. Khandker, 'Microfinance and Poverty Reduction: Evidence Using Panel Data from Bangladesh', *Journal of Development Economics* 76(2), 2005: 229–249.

16 In South Africa, Capitec is a leader in microlending to low-income earners. In the 1990s, low-income earners were charged as much as 30% per month for short-term, 30-day loans. However, recognising the need for more affordable credit, Capitec entered

this market and rapidly adjusted its model, reducing the rate to 18.5% per month. Today, the rate sits at between 13.0% and 28.5% per annum. This strategic shift not only enhanced client uptake but also underscored the transformative power of financial inclusion. By offering a more transparent and accessible alternative to traditional moneylenders, Capitec helped lower the effective cost of borrowing for underserved South Africans, contributing to broader economic participation and growth, evidencing the generalisable case.

17 H. Banna and M.R. Alam, 'Impact of Digital Financial Inclusion on ASEAN Banking Stability: Implications for the Post-Covid-19 Era', *Studies in Economics and Finance* 38(2), 2021: 504–523.

18 BlueEarth Capital, *BlueEarth Annual Impact Report 2023*, https://blueearth.capital/wp-content/uploads/2024/06/BlueEarth-Annual-Impact-Report-2023.pdf.

19 L-Y. Tay, H-T. Tai and G-S. Tan, 'Digital Financial Inclusion: A Gateway to Sustainable Development', *Heliyon* 8(6), 2022.

Chapter 6: A Pure Digital Plan

1 'Can CBA's Digital Bank Go Full Service', *DigFin*, 26 February 2018, https://www.digfingroup.com/cba/.

Chapter 7: Holding on for Dear Life

1 J. Barrett, 'Organizing in the Informal Economy: A Case Study of the Minibus Taxi Industry in South Africa', International Labour Organization, 2003, https://webapps.ilo.org/public/libdoc/ilo/2003/103B09_6_engl.pdf.

2 A. Ferguson, 'Why CBA's Ian Narev Had to "Retire"', *The Sydney Morning Herald*, 14 August 2017, https://www.smh.com.au/business/banking-and-finance/why-cbas-ian-narev-had-to-retire-20170814-gxvt2z.html. See also https://www.royalcommission.gov.au/banking/final-report.

Chapter 10: Building the Tyme Machine

1 H. de Soto, *The Mystery of Capital: Why Capitalism Triumphs in the West and Fails Everywhere Else* (New York: Basic Books, 2000); C.K. Prahalad, *The Fortune at the Bottom of the Pyramid: Eradicating Poverty through Profits*, revised edition (Philadelphia, PA: Wharton School Press, 2010).

2 Department of Agricultural and Consumer Economics, University of Illinois Urbana-Champaign, 25 May 2012. See also Federal Deposit Insurance Corporation (FDIC), *History of the Eighties: Lessons for the Future: Volume 1: An Examination of the Banking Crises of the 1980s and Early 1990s* (Washington, DC: FDIC, 1997), https://www.fdic.gov/system/files/2024-08/137_165.pdf.

3 A.C. Clarke, 'Voice on the Line' [interview], BBC Horizon, 1964.

NOTES

4 J. Rothfeder, *Driving Honda: Inside the World's Most Innovative Car Company* (New York: Portfolio, 2015).

5 A.C. Clarke, *Profiles of the Future: An Inquiry into the Limits of the Possible* (London: Harper & Row, 1962).

6 TymeBank, 'TymeBank Holdings Limited Annual Financial Statements', October 2024.

7 P. Ghemawat and J.L. Nueno, 'Zara: Fast Fashion', Harvard Business School Case 703-497, 2003, https://www.hbs.edu/faculty/Pages/item.aspx?num=29832.

8 'Pick n Pay Will Shut One in 10 Corporate Supermarkets', *Moneyweb*, 28 May 2024, www.moneyweb.co.za/news/companies-and-deals/pick-n-pay-will-shut-one-in-10-corporate-supermarkets/.

9 'FICO Survey: 56% of Filipinos Prefer to Use Digital Channels to Engage with Their Bank during Financial Hardship', FICO, 10 March 2021, https://www.fico.com/en/newsroom/fico-survey-56-filipinos-prefer-use-digital-channels-engage-their-bank-during-financial#:~:text=56%20percent%20of%20Filipino%20consumers,12%20percent%20use%20internet%20banking; Bangko Sentral ng Pilipinas, '2021 Financial Inclusion Survey', https://www.bsp.gov.ph/Inclusive%20Finance/Financial%20Inclusion%20Reports%20and%20Publications/2021/2021FISToplineReport.pdf.

10 Independent Communications Authority of South Africa, 'The State of the ICT Sector Report in South Africa', March 2023, https://www.icasa.org.za/legislation-and-regulations/state-of-ict-sector-report-2023-report; Statista, 'Share of People Who Used a Mobile Phone or the Internet to Send Money in the Past Year in South Africa as of 2022, by Gender', 2023, https://www.statista.com/statistics/1350310/share-of-people-using-online-banking-in-south-africa-by-gender/.

11 TymeBank, 'TymeBank Holdings Limited Annual Financial Statements', October 2024.

12 M. Goldman, N. Kleyn and L. Mazinter, 'TymeBank in 2019: Chasing the Millions', *Case Research Journal* 42(1), 2022.

13 See https://www.tiktok.com/@jhasminesmyll/video/7257135298801388805.

14 GoTyme, 'Victor's Big Move Signals a Banking Revolution', *ABS-CBN*, 23 December 2024, https://www.abs-cbn.com/news/business/2024/12/23/victor-s-big-move-signals-a-banking-revolution-1555.

15 GoTyme, 'Did You See That Video of Bridgetowne's Statue Walking in QC? We Finally Got Answers', SPOT.ph, 26 December 2024, https://www.spot.ph/newsfeatures/money/the-victor-bridgetowne-gotyme-5-million-users-adv-con.

Chapter 11: Going Beyond Borders

1 Startup Genome, *Global Startup Ecosystem Report 2022*, https://startupgenome.com.

2 R. Doherty, A. Mazhindu, M. Silberstein and T. Röder, 'The Growth Code: Go Global if You Can Beat Local', *McKinsey & Company*, 23 June 2023, https://www.mckinsey.

com/capabilities/strategy-and-corporate-finance/our-insights/the-strategy-and-corporate-finance-blog/the-growth-code-go-global-if-you-can-beat-local.

3 H. Marks, *The Most Important Thing: Uncommon Sense for the Thoughtful Investor* (New York: Columbia University Press, 2011).

4 M.E. Porter, *The Competitive Advantage of Nations* (New York: The Free Press, 1990).

5 R.S. Sisodia and J.N. Sheth, 'Competitive Markets and the Rule of Three', *Ivey Business Journal*, September/October 2002, https://iveybusinessjournal.com/publication/competitive-markets-and-the-rule-of-three/; F. Lafontaine and M.E. Slade, 'Defining Competition in Markets: Why and How?' *Journal of Economic Literature* 46(3), 2008: 570–578; L. Thi Thoan, V.T.N. Thuy and T.T. Long, 'Does Market Competition Make a Difference in Business Strategy for Listed Companies?' *Cogent Business & Management* 11(1), 2024, https://doi.org/10.1080/23311975.2024.2312591.

6 In fact, Tyme had previously ventured into Namibia. In 2013, they partnered with Pointbreak, a Namibian investment company, to build EBank. The service launched in 2014. However, following Tyme's acquisition by the Commonwealth Bank of Australia in 2015, they sold their 38.3% stake in EBank back to their partner, Pointbreak.

7 P. Ghemawat, 'Distance Still Matters: The Hard Reality of Global Expansion', *Harvard Business Review* 79(8), 2001: 137–147.

8 R. Kumar and M. Li, 'Digital Banking and Cross-Border Strategies', *Journal of International Business* 12(4), 2021: 45–67.

9 Doherty et al., 'The Growth Code'.

10 J. Haskel and S. Westlake, *Capitalism without Capital: The Rise of the Intangible Economy* (Princeton: Princeton University Press, 2018).

11 Google, Temasek and Bain & Company, 'e-Conomy SEA 2022: Through the Waves, towards a Sea of Opportunity', 2022, https://www.bain.com/globalassets/noindex/2022/e-conomy_sea_2022_report.pdf.

12 A-C. Paret Onorato, 'Southeast Asia's Economies Can Gain Most by Packaging Ambitious Reforms', *IMF Blog*, 25 March 2025, https://www.imf.org/en/Blogs/Articles/2025/03/25/southeast-asias-economies-can-gain-most-by-packaging-ambitious-reforms.

13 Bangko Sentral ng Pilipinas, 'Traversing New Heights: The Future Is Digital', 2023, https://www.bsp.gov.ph/PaymentAndSettlement/2023_Report_on_E-payments_Measurement.pdf.

14 'Mobile Payments with Digital Wallets: Statistics & Facts', Statista, 2024, https://www.statista.com/topics/4872/mobile-payments-worldwide/#:~:text=Digital%20payments%20involving%20the%20likes,percent%20between%202023%20and%202027.

15 Google, Temasek and Bain & Company, 'e-Conomy SEA 2022: Through the Waves, towards a Sea of Opportunity', 2022, https://www.bain.com/globalassets/noindex/2022/e-conomy_sea_2022_report.pdf.

16 D. Estrada and L. Cluff, 'Structural Analysis of Bank Competition and Performance:

Evidence from the Philippine Universal and Commercial Bank Group, 2011–2021', Presented at the BSP International Research Fair, 2023, https://www.bsp.gov.ph/Pages/ABOUT%20THE%20BANK/Events/By%20Year/2023/Research-Fair-2023/ppt/rcp2_presentation.pdf.

17 World Bank, *Financial Inclusion Lessons from World Bank Group Experience, Fiscal Years 2014–22*. Independent Evaluation Group. Washington, DC: World Bank, 2023, https://documents1.worldbank.org/curated/en/099305408252329233/pdf/SECBOS1e6ff9a00041b4261bcdc9c154a7b.pdf.

18 G.B. Sutrisno, 'Tyme Enters Indonesia as Part of SEA Expansion, Outlines Integration Plans', *Marketing-Interactive*, 20 January 2025, https://www.marketing-interactive.com/tyme-enters-indonesia-as-part-of-sea-expansion-outlines-integration-plans.

19 Sutrisno, 'Tyme Enters Indonesia as Part of SEA Expansion'.

20 Sutrisno, 'Tyme Enters Indonesia as Part of SEA Expansion'.

Chapter 12: Back from the Edge

1 A. Duckworth, *Grit: The Power of Passion and Perseverance* (New York: Scribner, 2016).

2 See https://www.tyme.com/tyme-x.

3 J. Clear, *Atomic Habits: Tiny Changes, Remarkable Results: An Easy & Proven Way to Build Good Habits & Break Bad Ones* (London: Penguin Random House, 2018).

4 There is an industry that tells stories of success backwards, which has spawned myths about the sources of success. The stories make for great reading, but most often confuse skill and luck. This makes for poor strategy. The evidence-based research distils skill from luck and finds firms that truly pull away from economic and industrial gravity, and that are in charge of their trajectory, are the true winners that should be studied, and include the likes of Amgen, Church's Fried Chicken, the DBS Group, Dutch Mining Services, Fujifilm, Medtronic and SingPost.

5 'Vietnam on List of Top Countries with the Most Engineering Graduates', *VietnamNet*, 18 June 2015, https://vietnamnet.vn/en/vietnam-on-list-of-top-countries-with-the-most-engineering-graduates-E133594.html#:~:text=graduating%20every%20year.-,VietNamNet%20Bridge%20%2D%20Vietnam%20ranks%2010th%20in%20a%20list%20of%20countries,graduates%20over%20past%20few%20decades.

6 See C. Larman and B. Vodde, *Scaling Lean & Agile Development: Thinking and Organizational Tools for Large-Scale Scrum* (Boston, MA: Addison-Wesley, 2008); C. Larman and B. Vodde, *Practices for Scaling Lean & Agile Development: Large, Multisite, and Offshore Product Development with Large-Scale Scrum* (Boston, MA: Addison-Wesley, 2010); C. Larman and B. Vodde, *Large-Scale Scrum: More with LeSS* (Boston, MA: Addison-Wesley, 2016).

7 A. Grant, *Hidden Potential: The Science of Achieving Greater Things* (New York: Viking, 2023).

NOTES

8 An SSL (Secure Sockets Layer) certificate is a digital certificate that authenticates the identity of a website and enables an encrypted connection link between a web server and a web browser.
9 'What is MultiX? How Has Tyme Built Our Serial Banks? Faster Expansion, Smarter Growth', https://www.youtube.com/watch?v=Xz9iOcsBxHs.

Chapter 15: Here's to the Crazy Ones

1 T.E. Lawrence, *Seven Pillars of Wisdom: A Triumph* (London: Jonathan Cape, 1926).
2 Corporate Research Foundation, *Top ICT Companies in South Africa* (Cape Town: Zebra Press, 2001).
3 'APAC Focus: Decoding the Digital Banking Potential in ASEAN', UBS, 2024, https://www.ubs.com/global/en/investment-bank/insights-and-data/2024/decoding-digital-banking-potential-asean.html.
4 W. Golding, *Lord of the Flies* (London: Penguin, 1954).
5 R. Bregman, *Humankind: A Hopeful History* (London: Bloomsbury Publishing, 2020).
6 D. Hume, *A Treatise of Human Nature*, edited by D.F. Norton and M.J. Norton (Oxford: Oxford University Press, [1739] 2007).
7 R.S. Zander and B. Zander, *The Art of Possibility: Practices in Leadership, Relationship and Passion* (New York: Penguin, 2002).
8 'SoFi Receives Regulatory Approval to Become a National Bank', SoFi, 18 January 2022, https://investors.sofi.com/news/news-details/2022/SoFi-Receives-Regulatory-Approval-to-Become-a-National-Bank/default.aspx.
9 '10 Million Members Now Getting Their Money Right with SoFi', SoFi, 17 December 2024, https://investors.sofi.com/news/news-details/2024/10-Million-Members-Now-Getting-Their-Money-Right-with-SoFi/default.aspx.
10 R. Rys, 'SoFi CEO Anthony Noto WG99 Is Reshaping Finance for the Digital Age', *Wharton Magazine*, Fall/Winter 2024, https://magazine.wharton.upenn.edu/issues/fall-winter-2024/sofi-ceo-anthony-noto-wg99-is-reshaping-finance-for-the-digital-age/.
11 David Vélez, 'Nubank 10 Years', *NU*, 11 May 2023, https://international.nubank.com.br/company/nubank-10-years-by-david-velez/.
12 'Africa's Macroeconomic Performance and Outlook: January 2025', *African Development Bank*, 14 February 2025, https://www.afdb.org/en/documents/africas-macroeconomic-performance-and-outlook-january-2025.
13 International Monetary Fund, 'World Economic Outlook Update: Global Growth: Divergent and Uncertain', January 2025, https://www.imf.org/en/Publications/WEO/Issues/2025/01/17/world-economic-outlook-update-january-2025.
14 J. Buchan, *The Gap in the Curtain* (Kelly Bray: House of Stratus, [1932] 2001).

Acknowledgements

This book owes its existence to the generosity of extraordinarily busy people who gave freely of their time.

Analysts, regulators, customers, past and present staff members, funders, shareholders, critics, collaborators and fans dug deep into their memories, often sharing difficult and sometimes painful recollections. The list of those who helped is too long to thank individually, yet we must single out Coenraad Jonker and Tjaart van der Walt for championing this book, and Nate Clarke, Dieter Botha and Rachel Freeman for the generosity of their time and the unfettered access they extended to us while hosting us in-country.

We also gained invaluable insights from movers and shakers in fintech and retail across Vietnam, the Philippines and Singapore, for which we remain deeply grateful.

As always, the patience, guidance and professionalism of the Pan Macmillan team – under managing director Terry Morris, publisher Andrea Nattrass, and editor Sally Hines – have been indispensable. Our thanks also go to the many people involved in producing, distributing, selling and marketing this book – your contributions are sincerely appreciated.

While we have benefited enormously from the generosity, insights and corrections of others, any remaining errors or omissions are entirely our own.

This story is far from over. As authors, we look forward to writing its next grand chapter – one we suspect is already taking shape in the minds of the Tyme leadership team.

Watch this space.

www.ingramcontent.com/pod-product-compliance
Ingram Content Group UK Ltd.
Pitfield, Milton Keynes, MK11 3LW, UK
UKHW041822241125
9145UKWH00033B/589